# THE
# EMDR COACH
## Practice with Confidence

*For my husband, Eric, for his unending support, patience, and stability. Thank you for growing with me and helping me find my true self. I love you always.*

www.theemdrcoach.com

# THE
## EMDR COACH
Practice with Confidence

*A journey of a thousand miles begins with a single step.*

*-Lao Tzu*

**THIS JOURNAL BELONGS TO:**

_____

_____

**MY THERAPIST:**

_____

_____

**DATE I STARTED EMDR THERAPY:**

_____

**DATE I GRADUATED EMDR THERAPY:**

_____

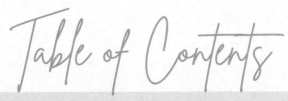

# Table of Contents

*Part One*

# WHAT'S IT ALL ABOUT?

*Introduction*

# WHAT TO EXPECT

An overview of what to expect during the EMDR Therapy Process

# *Introduction*

Welcome! I'm so excited that you're about to embark on your own healing journey with EMDR Therapy (Eye Movement Desensitization & Reprocessing.) Deciding to undergo trauma therapy is not always an easy decision, but it is certainly a courageous one. It's completely normal to feel scared, anxious, or not sure what to expect when you start the process. The definition of courage is to feel scared but do it anyway.

## HOW TO USE THIS JOURNAL

This journal is designed to be a guide to support you as you undergo EMDR Therapy with a Licensed Mental Health Practitioner who is formally trained in EMDR Therapy. This journal is NOT intended to be a replacement for EMDR Therapy, and is not considered EMDR Therapy as a standalone. There are sections for notes throughout this workbook to encourage you to make note of what's important, insights you have, or questions you'd like to ask your therapist.

## THIS JOURNAL IS INTENDED TO:

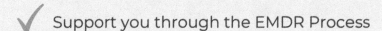

- ✓ Support you through the EMDR Process

- ✓ Help you be an active participant of your own healing journey

- ✓ Increase mindfulness, intention, and self awareness through reflections and exercises

- ✓ Explain how the process works so you know what to expect

- ✓ Help you achieve your treatment goals faster

The information in this journal includes psychoeducation to inform you about the process and worksheets to help clarify your goals and increase your self awareness. This structure and organization can help you stay focused so you can overcome anxiety, depression, PTSD or other trauma-related conditions.

# Introduction

When embarking on your journey with EMDR Therapy, it's important to remember:

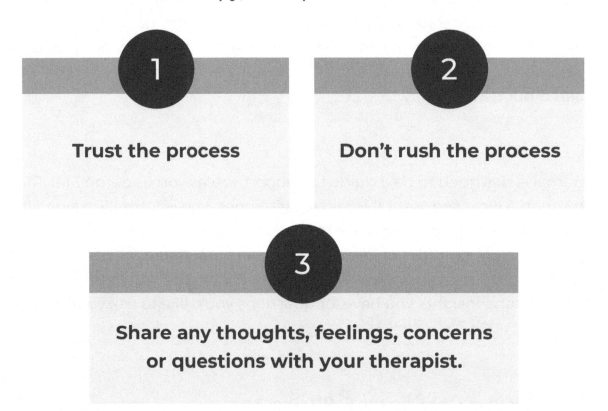

**1**

**Trust the process**

**2**

**Don't rush the process**

**3**

**Share any thoughts, feelings, concerns or questions with your therapist.**

Your therapist is there to help and guide you, so if you need clarification, have a concern, or something isn't working for you, let your therapist know! EMDR can be modified to suit your individual needs, so you can't do this wrong. Communication is the best way to help your therapist help you.

Every single person is different, which means that your experience may vary from someone else's. Many individuals want to jump right into the reprocessing part of the therapy and skip over the slowing down parts (preparation work). Slowing down may feel frustrating when you just want to feel better, but doing so is necessary and, sometimes, IS the work that needs to be done more than the reprocessing of traumatic experiences. Although you may want to jump right to the reprocessing, slowing down first will help you get the full impact of the therapy and help you achieve your treatment goals.

# WHAT TO EXPECT

## WHAT IS EMDR?

EMDR stands for *Eye Movement Desensitization and Reprocessing* and is a trauma informed, integrative approach to psychotherapy. This means that it incorporates some of the best approaches, tools and techniques from several different therapies into one comprehensive mega-therapy.

This flexible and integrative framework helps an individual heal from past experiences that are contributing to their present day symptoms, while gaining hope and confidence for the future.

The focus of EMDR is on what happened to you, not what is "wrong" with you. This means that rather than just managing your symptoms, you can finally be free of them *for good*.

EMDR is also *not* just for trauma, but has been proven effective for performance enhancement for athletes, entrepreneurs, relationships, and more. While traditionally it works on healing from the past, it also can help with enhancing hope and confidence for the future.

## PROCESSING VS. TALK THERAPY

EMDR is quite different than talk therapy. This may feel weird to some, especially those who have been in traditional talk therapy in the past. With EMDR, you do not have to come up with "stuff" to talk about at each session. In fact, that can be counterproductive to the EMDR process.

EMDR is helpful when just talking about something is not enough. Talking is a very cognitive practice; however, just because we "know" something in our minds does not mean our body gets the message. Feeling stuck is a common experience for survivors of trauma because they might know cognitively that they are safe, but their body does not feel safe.

In this journal, whenever we refer to "processing" or "reprocessing", we are referring to phases 3-6 of EMDR Therapy. Processing means that you are taking an experience that has not been properly digested by your brain and re-creating it in an ideal, <u>safe</u> learning environment.

# WHAT TO EXPECT

This ideal learning state helps your brain to properly digest the memory so it no longer stays in its raw, natural state. The negative thoughts, emotions and sensations will be gone, and you will only retain information from that experience that is useful to you now.

This means that situations in the present moment will no longer trigger experiences from the past. Instead, you will be in control of how you think, feel and act.

## HOW DOES EMDR WORK?

EMDR is based on "Adaptive Information Processing", meaning that present day symptoms stem from our life experiences. These present day symptoms can be thought of as *re-livings*.  When we experience a re-living, something from the past is impacting how we think, feel or behave in the present, because our brain thinks the past IS present. EMDR helps to reprocess the past experiences that get triggered in the present, and turn them into autobiographical memories.

You do not have to have a visual past experience to be able to do EMDR therapy. For some individuals, especially those with developmental and attachment trauma, the pain may also stem from the memories they do not have (neglect), or from experiences that happened when they were too young to remember. The mind may not remember, but the body does, and that's how these re-livings show up in one's present day life.

EMDR also helps to create experiences *now* that you didn't get when you were younger through the use of imaginal resourcing and visualization.  These imaginal exercises, combined with the bilateral stimulation that EMDR is based upon, help these experiences fully integrate into your mind and body.

Imagining something has the same effect on the brain as if it's actually happening.  If you imagine something negative, you feel worse.  If you imagine something positive, like these imaginal resourcing exercises, you feel better. The bilateral stimulation then helps to enhance the positive responses you get from these exercises and strengthens your ability to access the positive feelings more easily when they're recalled.

# WHAT TO EXPECT

## WHAT IS BILATERAL STIMULATION?

Bilateral stimulation (BLS) is an important component of EMDR Therapy. BLS is a form of stimuli that involves following a rhythmic pattern of alternating left/right movements from one side of the body to the other. This may be in the form of eye-movements, audio tones, or tactile taps. You can expect the speed of the BLS movements to be slow for preparation work (phase 2) and faster for reprocessing work (phase 4).

There have been several studies that are beginning to show just how and why the use of BLS is a significant factor in processing trauma through the use of EEG and functional MRI technologies. Some of these findings demonstrate how the use of BLS creates significant differences in the level of neurobiological activation vs. talk therapy alone (talking vs. EMDR)

## THE THREE TYPES

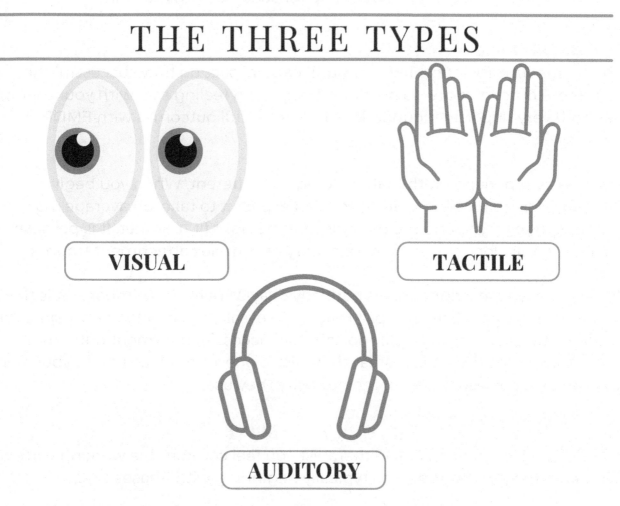

VISUAL

TACTILE

AUDITORY

*Introduction*
# WHAT TO EXPECT

## SET YOURSELF UP FOR SUCCESS

It's important to have realistic expectations when beginning EMDR Therapy. EMDR helps to resolve traumatic stress related to adverse life experiences. It cannot, however, cure medical and neurological conditions with an organic basis.

EMDR is meant to be done with intention so you get the most out of it. Before beginning treatment, think about what your goals are for starting EMDR. What are you hoping to get out of the process? Do you want to do full comprehensive treatment (going back to the earliest life experiences that are connected to present day triggers and symptoms) or do you want to focus only on symptom reduction (staying with the more recent experiences and not going into earlier past)? Be sure to discuss your intentions and expectations for treatment with your therapist so that you can be set up for success from the start!

## FINDING THE RIGHT FIT

The therapeutic relationship has a significant impact on how successful the treatment outcomes are, so building rapport and feeling safe with your therapist are both **very** important foundations for successful outcomes with EMDR Therapy.

Everyone's experience with EMDR is uniquely different. When you begin working with an EMDR therapist, you can expect it to take, on average, 1-3 sessions to see if you and the therapist are the right fit together. It is possible that it can take longer if you have a history of complex attachment trauma.

If the fit doesn't feel right, that is perfectly okay! What's **most** important is that you work with an EMDR therapist that you feel safe and connected to, since the therapeutic relationship is so important for successful treatment outcomes. What makes any therapist a **great** therapist is one who can attune to your own individual needs, regardless of the modality they use.

## GETTING STARTED WITH YOUR THERAPIST

Once you have found an EMDR therapist you feel comfortable working with, you will begin the process together, typically beginning with Phases 1 & 2.

*Introduction*

# WHAT TO EXPECT

Remember, that just because you're not doing eye-movements or tapping doesn't mean you're not doing EMDR. This is a common misconception among many.

The use of bilateral stimulation begins in phase 2, but the reprocessing of traumatic stress using eye-movements (or other forms of bilateral stimulation) does not begin until phases 4. History taking and preparation build a solid foundation for the reprocessing work, and it's ALL part of EMDR Therapy.

In cases of complex/chronic trauma, you may experience longer preparation stages, which still is ALL part of EMDR Therapy.  If the preparation work is longer than you expected, ask your therapist! It's normal to have questions, and communication about expectations helps your overall progress.

## REPROCESSING

Once you begin the reprocessing phases, you may notice:
- fatigue after your session (your brain is doing a lot of work!)
- increase in agitation
- increase in anxiety
- nightmares or vivid dreams
- other short term discomfort

This is common during treatment, but it's always important to make note of what comes up between sessions and bring that up with your therapist. If/When this does occur, it's also helpful to use the resources you created in phase 2 to help stabilize the discomfort in between sessions. You can use the **TICES Log** in part 2 of this journal to help keep track of what occurs in between sessions and discuss with your therapist.

EMDR is based on the 3 prong approach: past, present, and future. After you clear out the past memories you have identified with your therapist, it's important to make sure you also process the present day triggers and desired future outcomes. This is what helps to solidify your progress and prevents symptoms from coming back.

# WHAT TO EXPECT

As with all trauma work, EMDR can be emotionally intense. At all times, your therapist will be there to help you remember that you are safe in their office and to gently support you through any difficult parts of the process.

### GETTING READY TO GRADUATE

At the completion of the EMDR Process, you can expect to have achieved the goals that you and your therapist first established when creating your treatment plan, as well as other goals that you may have added along the way. These goals may include resolutions of certain symptoms that you struggled with at the beginning of therapy,

Many individuals who have completed EMDR Therapy report having increased compassion for themselves, as well as more compassion for others.

It's helpful to review your treatment goals toward the end of your work and use the *Reprocessing Reflections* worksheet (included in Part 2) to make note of the ways your life has improved, as well as identify anything else you'd like to work on before you graduate from EMDR Therapy.

The following section will go into more detail about the 8 phases of EMDR so you have a more comprehensive idea of what to expect.

EMDR does not change the facts of your life, but it can change how you feel and how you live your life going forward.

- *Laurell Parnell*

*Step-by-Step*

# THE 8 PHASES

In this section, we will walk you through each of the eight phases of EMDR therapy and explain them in greater detail. This section is designed to give you a greater understanding of the process so you know what to expect throughout your journey.

# Step-by-Step
# THE 8 PHASES

The Standard Protocol for EMDR is based upon the 8 phase, 3 Prong Approach (past, present, future). This includes clearing out past experiences, desensitizing present day triggers and installing future desirable outcomes. Including the present and future time periods in the processing helps to solidify and strengthen the new connections your brain has made to positive associations.

The Standard Protocol for EMDR is the first line of defense; *however,* you and your therapist may determine that a modified approach is needed instead. This is normal and all part of the process, *especially in cases of attachment and developmental trauma.* For clients with attachment and developmental trauma, taking time to build a solid therapeutic relationship is super important, and is considered part of the Preparation Phase of EMDR Therapy.

The therapeutic relationship can have a significant impact on how successful the treatment outcomes are, so building rapport and feeling safe with your therapist are both very important prerequisites for the reprocessing phases of EMDR Therapy.

Let's break down each of the 8 phases in more detail so you know what to expect.

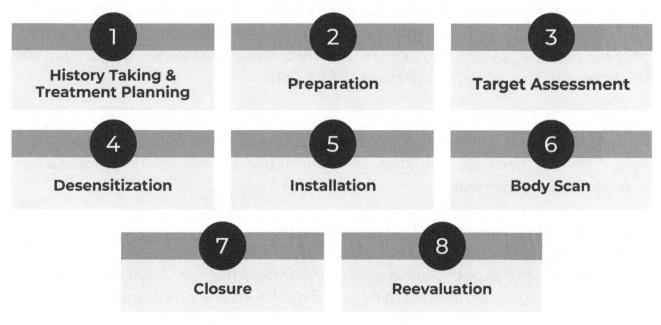

1 History Taking & Treatment Planning

2 Preparation

3 Target Assessment

4 Desensitization

5 Installation

6 Body Scan

7 Closure

8 Reevaluation

# Step-by-Step
# THE 8 PHASES

## PHASE 1: HISTORY TAKING AND TREATMENT PLANNING

History taking focuses on getting an understanding of why you're coming in for treatment, how trauma is currently affecting you and what your goals are for successful outcomes.

During this phase, your therapist will identify your present day symptoms, (anxiety, angry outbursts, depression, etc.) and then help you to connect them to other life experiences where they originated. Your therapist will then create a *Target Sequence Plan*, which is a map of memories from the past that are connected to present day triggers, as well as future desirable actions (ways that you want to be able to respond to those triggers in the future). This target sequence plan lays the groundwork for the 3 Prong Approach that EMDR Therapy is based upon.

During this phase, your therapist may also assess for levels of dissociation (which is very common in survivors of trauma.). All of this information from history taking and assessment will help your therapist formulate an individualized treatment plan that best meets your needs.

It's important to note that you do NOT have to tell the whole story of past memories during History Taking, because EMDR is not talk therapy. During history taking, you and your therapist will connect present day symptoms to past experiences, but not go into the stories of those past experiences. That will be done with the reprocessing stages of EMDR.

## PHASE 2: PREPARATION

Preparation, also known as the resourcing/stabilization phase, is a crucial part of EMDR Therapy because it builds a solid foundation for successful reprocessing of traumatic experiences.

The goals of this phase of EMDR therapy are to:
- build a solid therapeutic alliance with your therapist
- review what to expect during treatment and address any concerns you have
- learn relaxation techniques to help you deal with any emotional disturbance

# THE 8 PHASES

- work through any barriers, like dissociation, that can effect your readiness for reprocessing.

In order to process our stressful life experiences, we have to be able to feel the emotions and sensations associated with them. This phase of EMDR helps to establish a layer of safety so that feeling your feelings won't be SO overwhelming. Will it be uncomfortable? Sure. But the preparation work in this phase helps to ease that discomfort as much as possible.

This phase is also when you may begin using some of the bilateral stimulation (eye movements, taps, etc.) based on your own individual treatment plan, to pair with the relaxation resources you are learning. Examples of resourcing activities include: the container, calm state, meditation exercises, breathing exercises, light stream, ego state work, installing attachment figures, etc.

Creating resources and techniques is not a one-size-fits-all approach, so literally *anything* can be a resource. If one of the tools or exercises does not work for you, that's okay! You and your therapist will work together to find the ones that do. You can't do this wrong!

For individuals with a complex history of trauma and high levels of dissociation, phase 2 may take longer, depending on how well resourced they are prior to starting EMDR Therapy.

In cases of developmental/attachment trauma, resourcing may even be the main focal point of the treatment because this phase helps give you what you did not get when you were younger and fill in those developmental gaps. Again, there's no one-size-fits-all approach when it comes to EMDR. What is most important is that YOU get what YOU need to heal.

## PHASE 3: TARGET ASSESSMENT

After you have identified a list of experiences and created a safety net, you & your therapist will decide which experience (aka "target") to start with. Your therapist will then ask a specific set of questions about this experience to establish the ideal learning state for you to process the experience.

# THE 8 PHASES

This phase is supposed to be relatively quick, so you want to avoid getting into a conversation. The goal is to activate your nervous system to the optimal level of arousal needed for reprocessing to take place. The seven questions your therapist will ask are:

**What Image/(or other sensory component)** represents the worst part of the issue/experience?

**NC (Negative Cognition)** What do you believe about yourself when you think about this experience?

**PC (Positive Cognition)** What you wish you could think about yourself instead (even if you don't believe it all)?

**VoC (Validity of Cognition):** How true do you believe that positive thought, on a scale from 1-7, 1 is not at all and 7 is totally true?

**Emotions:** What emotions do you experience as you bring your attention to that experience?

**SuD (subjective units of disturbance):** How disturbing is the experience, from 0 to 10, 0 is not at all, 10 is the worst?

**Body Scan:** What sensations do you feel in your body as your focus on this experience?

## PHASE 4: DESENSITIZATION

After the components of the experience have been established, you will begin reprocessing the traumatic experience with bilateral stimulation. During this phase, you do not have to actively think of anything. Just notice whatever happens. It might be a thought, an emotion, or a sensation in your body, or you may recall another memory altogether. You can't do this wrong, just let your mind and body go wherever they need to go. The goal is to observe and just notice whatever happens next. After your therapist stops the BLS, they will then ask "what do you notice now? What did you observe? Etc."

# THE 8 PHASES

Again, the feedback you share with your therapist should be brief. You want to avoid getting into too much talking in between sets, because talking can take your brain out of the processing mode.

Your therapist will check in from time to time and recheck the level of disturbance related to the experience you are working on. These rating scales are designed to keep track of your progress.  Answer as honestly as you can, knowing there is no right or wrong answer. The honest answer is the right answer because that is what helps you heal.

*An important note for people pleasers. Do not say what you think your therapist wants you to say. It's not your job to "do EMDR correctly" and make your therapist happy. This is YOUR process, so don't be afraid to speak up if something isn't clicking for you.  The only "wrong" answer is the one that does not accurately reflect what you are really feeling.*

## PHASE 5: INSTALLATION
During installation, you will be reinforcing the new positive beliefs about yourself in relation to the memory. Your therapist will ask, "What belief do you have about yourself now in relation to the experience?", as well as how true those words feel to you now on a scale from 0 (totally false) to 7 (totally true). Respond with whatever feels true to you. Your therapist will then proceed to do more sets of BLS until that number is the highest that it can be.

## PHASE 6: BODY SCAN
The body scan is to make sure there is no leftover trauma stored in the body. Your therapist will ask you to bring your attention back to the experience that you first started working on and ask you to scan your body from head to toe. As you scan your body, check for any tension or discomfort that you notice.  This phase is designed to make sure that there is no residual unprocessed material, and if there is, gives space to clear it out.

# THE 8 PHASES

## PHASE 7: CLOSURE

This happens at the end of every processing session, even if you're not finished with the experience you began working on. It's quite common to not clear out a target in one session, (unless you're doing EMDR Intensives.) The goal of the closure phase is to help bring your nervous system back to a calm state and leave the session with all the tools you need to function in between sessions.

## PHASE 8: REEVALUATION

Re-Evaluation occurs at the beginning of every session when the previous one ended with an incomplete target. The goal of this phase is to reactivate the experience to an optimal level of arousal , so you can continue with the reprocessing.

## THE 3 PRONG APPROACH

Remember that EMDR is based on the 3 Prong Approach. After you clear out the past memories, remember, you're not done yet! Processing the present day triggers and the future scenarios helps to solidify your progress and decrease the likelihood of your symptoms coming back.

## A MODIFIED APPROACH

It's not uncommon that for some individuals, the Standard Protocol may not be the best approach.  For example, for some individuals, starting with the earliest memories may feel way too overwhelming.  You and your therapist may decide to start with more recent events to ease you into the process.  In other instances, your therapist may start with the future scenarios first, so you can  build up confidence that this approach can work for you.  In cases of complex and/or chronic trauma, the attachment focused approach or early trauma protocol may be better suited.

EMDR Therapy is a flexible framework that guides trauma therapy. There are SO many different approaches to EMDR Therapy, so it's always best to ask your therapist which approach you're doing.  This helps you understand your own treatment plan and avoid concerns that you or your therapist are "doing it wrong".

# *Summary*
# 8 PHASES OF EMDR

| PHASE | GOALS | TASKS |
|---|---|---|
| **HISTORY TAKING** | Get a full history from client, (past, present, future) and assess client's needs to be able to achieve treatment goals. | • Complete AIP History Taking, using floatback.<br>• Identify clinical themes and memories connected to each theme.<br>• Psychoeducation on the EMDR process<br>• Screen for dissociation<br>• Complete Case Conceptualization |
| **RESOURCING** | To help clients achieve stabilization necessary to maintain dual awareness for reprocessing of traumatic material | • Psychoeducation on the window of tolerance<br>• Teach sufficient resourcing skills/exercises for dual awareness<br>• Address concerns & obtain consent for working on traumatic memories<br>• BLS Speed: Slow |
| **TARGET ASSESSMENT** | Stimulate the nervous system by focus on key components of traumatic memory. | • Utilize 7 Magic Questions to prepare memory (Image, NC, PC, VoC, Emotion, SuD, Body Scan) |
| **DESENSITIZATION** | Desensitize traumatic memory & reprocess related material to a SuD of 0/ecological 1 | • Use BLS to desensitize and reprocess traumatic material<br>• Assess for progress via client feedback in between sets.<br>• Monitor for looping/stuck processing<br>• Monitoring for dual awareness<br>• BLS Speed: Fast |
| **INSTALLATION** | Increase the VoC related to the PC to 7. | • Determine if PC from phase 3 is still appropriate<br>• Use BLS to increase the VoC<br>• BLS Speed: Fast |
| **BODY SCAN** | Clear any disturbance still left in the body related to the identified experience. | • Using BLS for any disturbance still identified in the body until clear<br>• BLS Speed: Fast |
| **CLOSURE** | To ensure client stability before ending a session:<br>• Address any client needs for in between sessions.<br>• Remind client what to expect in between sessions. | • Utilization of identified resources during phase 2 creating new resources as needed.<br>• Closure is done at the end of every reprocessing session. |
| **REEVALUATION** | Keep track of progress in between sessions. | • Global assessment of functioning<br>• Target specific assessment<br>• Re-access memory of incomplete target (Image, Emotion, SuD, Body Scan) |

*Understanding Your Past*

# HOW MEMORIES WORK

In this chapter we define the four types of memories: implicit, explicit, episodic and semantic. This will help you to conceptualize your own experiences (or lack thereof) and begin identifying potential targets for the reprocessing phases of EMDR Therapy.

# HOW MEMORIES WORK

Memories are a funny thing. We often think of memories as being able to recall something visually in our mind from an experience in the past. But that's just ONE type of memory (called explicit memories).

In order to understand more about how EMDR Therapy works, it may be helpful to understand the different types of memories there are, especially if you struggle to remember anything traumatic happening to you.

## IMPLICIT MEMORIES

Implicit memories are habits that do not require conscious thought. An implicit memory is something that is recalled unconsciously, without any intention. It is often a procedural memory, meaning it's a remembered process, such as riding a bike or learning how to walk.

Implicit memories are usually not memories that you can remember verbally. Think about it - when you stand up and walk every day, are you consciously remembering the time you took your first steps when you were a baby? Or do you just get up and start moving?

One way that implicit memory relates to childhood trauma is when a baby experiences an unmet Attachment Cry. This is a form of developmental trauma, in which a baby's cries for help were not responded to on a consistent basis. Once that baby grows into adulthood, they can be labeled as "attention-seeking" or be diagnosed with Borderline Personality Disorder, because they become very emotionally dysregulated whenever they perceive being abandoned/not responded to.

That "attention-seeking" behavior is an implicit memory - an action that was learned through repetition. That baby's attempts for attachments were unmet, so baby learned to cry and act out to get a caregiver's attention. This process became encoded into implicit memory because it is remembered automatically and without intention.

# HOW MEMORIES WORK

## EXPLICIT MEMORIES
Explicit memories, on the other hand, are memories that you either consciously choose to recall OR that come into your awareness through association (without intention).

For example, you may choose to think about the time you went on vacation with your family when feeling nostalgic. Or the smell of cookies may remind you of a time you would bake cookies with your Grandma.

Explicit Memories can be broken down into two types of memories: Episodic Memory and Semantic Memory.

## EPISODIC MEMORY
Episodic memories are typically memories that relate to your own personal experiences. Think of this type of memory as an "episode" in your brain. These types of memories can include remembering when your child was born, the day you got married, your first day of school, etc.

An episodic memory is NOT always "accurate". Two people can have two different episodic memories of the same event. This is because episodic memories are based on perception and associated emotions.

## SEMANTIC MEMORY
Semantic memories are memories that are like "facts" in our brains that we have learned, but don't relate to our own personal lives much. An example of this would be remembering that the sky is blue or the grass is green.

## WHICH MEMORIES DOES EMDR WORK WITH?
EMDR works on implicit memories and episodic memories.

During Phase 1 of EMDR Therapy, triggers are explored. First identifying the trigger helps the therapist guide you to the memory or memories that are be associated with that trigger.

# HOW MEMORIES WORK

Remember that cookie example from before? The smell of cookies is the trigger and the associated memory is the time with your Grandma.

Let's use another example of an unprocessed episodic memory involving a veteran who has combat PTSD. The sound of a car backfiring may trigger a flashback from combat, including the images, emotions and behaviors associated with that experience. In this instance, the sound of the car backfiring was the trigger associated with the past.

We can tell this is an unprocessed memory because of the way the veteran responds when hearing the sound of the car. If the memory were processed, he might be reminded of the experience, but would not be flooded with unwanted images, emotions, and acting like he was back in combat.

Let's look at another example of unprocessed memories of relational trauma. In this instance, there are two partners who get into an argument with one another, and the argument is the trigger.

That argument may trigger feelings of abandonment and behaviors in one (or both) of the partners, such as withdrawing and becoming emotionally shut down, or going into a state of panic at the idea of their partner leaving them.

Having an understanding of the types of memories you're working with in EMDR Therapy can help you determine your approach in your treatment plan.

For individuals with a history of complex / chronic trauma, it may be difficult to pinpoint specific memories. You may find yourself thinking, "there were so many times, how do I begin to focus on one? They all seemed to blur together." Your therapist will help you narrow it down or perhaps focus on a period of time instead of a specific memory.

History taking (phase 1 of EMDR) is designed to help you pinpoint the memories that are contributing to your present day symptoms. If you can't remember something, that's okay. Your therapist is there to guide you through the history taking process to help you uncover what from your past is associated with your current struggles.

*Defining Trauma*

# AM I TRAUMATIZED?

Trauma is a subjective experience. Read on to learn more about the different types of trauma and how to determine if your past experiences are affecting your present.

"Trauma is not what happens to us, but what we hold inside of us in the absence of an empathetic witness."

*- Peter Levine*

# THREE TYPES OF TRAUMA

Our society commonly thinks of trauma as a major event, or something that's glaringly obvious as traumatic; however, trauma is better defined as not a specific event, but rather, as a perceived experience. How you individually experience something (how your nervous system responds) and who or what helped you through, can determine how affected you are by it later on in life.

Trauma can be anything that is too much for too long, too little for too long, or too much in a short period of time. The chart below is an example of three different ways to categorize trauma, but keep in mind, trauma is ANYTHING that exceeds your ability to cope.

The reason that we break down trauma into these 3 categories is simply because it helps you & your therapist to create a treatment plan that is specific to your own individual needs.

| 1 | 2 | 3 |
|---|---|---|
| **ACUTE TRAUMA** | **CHRONIC TRAUMA** | **COMPLEX TRAUMA** |
| When something happens suddenly. Typically a single incident experience. | When exposed to an ongoing traumatic experience environment over time. | When exposed to several different traumatic experiences or a combination of acute and chronic traumas. |
| Car accident, sexual assault, natural disaster, medical event. | Childhood abuse/neglect, domestic violence, bullying, sexual abuse, living in poverty or extreme conditions, war. | Attachment trauma (ruptures in connection with caregivers in the earliest years of life) and a combination of acute & chronic situations. |

*Treatment Plan*

You and your therapist will decide on the best treatment plan approach based on your goals for therapy and the type of trauma you have experienced.

# AM I TRAUMATIZED?

## HOW DO I KNOW IF I'VE EXPERIENCED TRAUMA?

Trauma does NOT have to be a significant, big event. Trauma is anything that is too much for too long, too little for too long, or too much in a short period of time and exceeds our nervous system's ability to cope.

## ADVERSE CHILDHOOD EXPERIENCES

The Adverse Childhood Experiences Study was a ground-breaking study which found a very strong correlation between experiences of abuse, neglect and household dysfunction and an adult's overall physical, mental and emotional health.

This study demonstrated that adversity in childhood may lead to an increased chance for disease and a lower mortality rate. Beyond just physical health, individuals who scored high on this questionnaire are MUCH more likely to struggle with varying mental health conditions. To take the free assessment for yourself, visit: *www.peacefullivingmentalhealthcounseling.com/traumaquiz*

## THE EFFECT OF NEGLECT

Trauma is not just what happens to you. It is also what <u>didn't</u> happen to you. From the earliest years of life, we need a competent, caring figure help us regulate our emotions, which in turn, helps our nervous system develop appropriately. If the development of our nervous system was affected during our earliest years of life, we're much more likely to develop PTSD/CPTSD later on in life.

Neglect is a pervasive, and often overlooked, form of trauma. It is often referred to by many therapists as "small T" traumas. And these types of experiences are often so subtle and quick, that they goes unnoticed to the untrained eye. But these small, subtle experiences build up over time and, combined, have a big impact. At a young age, this can be very damaging, because we don't yet have the capacity to understand what it is that we are feeling.

We just know that it's awful and uncomfortable and we don't know what to do about it. Without someone teaching us that what we're feeling is normal and showing us how to regulate those feelings, we're left to subconsciously make

# AM I TRAUMATIZED?

assumptions of ourselves, such as "I'm not good enough", "There must be something wrong with me", etc.

If you think neglect wouldn't affect a child, go on YouTube and search "still face experiment." It's hard to watch, but it proves just how painful it feels for a child whose attempts at connection are rejected without any repair afterwards.

## THE IMPORTANCE OF SUPPORT

More likely than not, all of us at some point in our lives have experienced a significant stressor or loss. But the actual event does not always correlate with how it affects someone. Two people may experience the exact same event and respond differently to it. There there are so many factors at play that determine how someone perceives an experience, including their own neurological makeup, proximity to the event, genetics, generational trauma history, personal frames of reference, etc.

And it's often not just what happened to us, but <u>who</u> was there for us afterwards, that can influence whether or not we will be affected by something long term. Many studies show that individuals who feel supported after a distressing experience are less effected long term versus individuals who feel lonely and unsupported.

A recent study from 2018 by E.E. et. al found that there was a very strong correlation between loneliness and adverse health conditions, both physically and mentally.

## ARE YOU LONELY?

Loneliness is a perceived experience. This means that you can be surrounded by people but still feel lonely. Or you can live alone but still feel connected to your environment.

If you're curious about the effects of loneliness on your own health and wellness, the **UCLA Loneliness Scale** may help give you some insight. This is a self-report assessment that measures your own subjective feelings of loneliness.

# AM I TRAUMATIZED?

A quick Google search should pull up a free and easy way to view the assessment and take it for yourself. The higher the score, the higher the likelihood that your physical and mental health may be at risk.

This is one of the reasons why seeing a therapist can be so important. A therapist can provide support and a space for you to process your thoughts and emotions so you don't have to do it alone. Seeing a therapist doesn't mean there's something wrong with you. It means that you're human because we ALL need support.

## OTHER HELPFUL ASSESSMENTS

In addition to the ones mentioned above, there are many different assessment tools that your therapists may use to help get a better understanding of your current symptoms and to help establish the best possible treatment plan. Some of these assessments may include:

**Dissociative Experiences Scale (DES-II):** To assess for levels of dissociation

**The Multidimensional Inventory of Dissociation (MID):** A more in-depth assessment for dissociation.

**The Impact of Events Scale (Revised):** To assess for PTSD and the different sub-types of PTSD.

**The Adult Attachment Interview Protocol (Kaplan & Main):** To get a feel for your earliest relationships from childhood and how your attachment style developed

**Adverse Childhood Experiences Questionnaire** (referenced on p. 33): Visit *www.peacefullivingmentalhealthcounseling.com/traumaquiz* to take the quiz.

"Trauma is not just what happens to you.
It's what happens inside of you as a result of what happens to you."

- *Garbor Mate*

*Dissociation*

# THE TRAUMA & DISSOCIATION CONNECTION

Dissociation goes hand in hand with traumatic experiences. Read on to learn about the varying levels of dissociation and what you need to know before processing traumatic experiences.

"The attempt to escape from pain, is what creates more pain."

- Gabor Mate

# TRAUMA & DISSOCIATION

## WHAT IS DISSOCIATION?

Dissociation is the disconnection between a person's thoughts, emotions, sensations, sense of self and/or personal history. Think of it as the act of compartmentalizing an experience or a part of yourself, like storing it away in a trunk in your mind. That experience is an isolated fragment that was never properly "learned", so it never became part of your story.

Compartmentalizing upsetting memories helps you continue to function in daily life; however, it becomes dysfunctional when those dissociated parts get triggered and impede on your daily life and ability to function. A trigger causes the trunk in your mind to pop open, without your awareness, and affects you without you having any control over it.

There are certain levels of dissociation that are typical in day-to-day life. Ever get that feeling when you're driving somewhere that you've driven a million times before, so your mind wanders? That's a form of dissociation. You disconnect from reality and go somewhere else in your mind, so your actions in the present (driving) are on autopilot. Dissociation becomes problematic when it affects your ability to function and fully experience life. This includes being able to feel and regulate your emotions, connect intimately with others, live in the moment, remember important information, etc.

## DISCONNECT TO PROTECT

Dissociation is often referred to as the freeze or shutdown response (*see the chapter on Understanding Your Nervous System, which goes into more detail about this*). When something traumatic happens to us, we disconnect from ourselves and our inner experience. Dissociation typically occurs when we cannot fight back or run away (sympathetic nervous system), so we escape to our inner world (dorsal vagal shutdown) as a way to mentally escape from the painful situation. We shut down, involuntarily, as a survival mechanism.

Peter Levine discusses in his book, "Waking The Tiger", *(an excellent book on trauma)* about an impala getting chased by a lion. If the impala gets caught by the lion, the impala plays dead and disconnects from its body.

# TRAUMA & DISSOCIATION

This occurs because the impala believes it is now going to die, so it disconnects from the felt sense so it does not have the feel the pain of the attack.

If you think about this from the perspective of a trauma survivor, such as someone who experienced or witnessed any type of abuse, or was living in a chronically emotionally neglectful environment, disconnecting from the felt sense is actually a very helpful way in which the brain responds. Disconnecting from emotions or physical sensations, helps the individual to *not feel* overwhelming or constant pain, just like the impala when caught by the lion.

What happens, though, if the impala gets a chance to escape from the lion? What animals typically do is quite physically shake it off, which helps them discharge the energy from their sympathetic nervous system. That discharge of energy helps them complete the nervous system response to a traumatic event so they can move on and continue to function in the wild. YouTube *"Polar Bear Shaking Off Trauma",* which demonstrates this process.

For us humans, however, we may stay stuck in that dissociated state,. This stops us from releasing the stored up sympathetic energy, which would allow us to complete the nervous system response. We survived, but a part of us is still stuck in the past and has not realized that the danger is over, so we continue to stay in a state of disconnection to avoid pain.

Picture it like revving a car engine in neutral. All that energy from the engine is stored up but you have to pop the car into drive to release it. If that car never gets popped into drive, all that stored energy stays stuck and can eventually cause the car to malfunction or breakdown. Even though the dissociation was helpful in the past, it may now causes you to feel stuck and not able to fully function in the present.

## WHAT DOES DISSOCIATION LOOK LIKE?

In its most severe form, dissociation can present as Dissociative Identity Disorder (previously known as Multiple Personality Disorder). In these cases, an individual has two or more personalities, each with their own identity and perceptions. However, dissociation can also present in many other ways.

# TRAUMA & DISSOCIATION

*Dissociation*

Dissociation is a spectrum, and can vary in intensity and presentation. A hallmark of possible dissociation is if you've been in therapy for an average of 7 years and have made little to no progress. Dissociation can often look like treatment resistant depression (or *Dorsal Vagal Shutdown*, more on this in Chapter 6. )

The types of dissociation include: depersonalization (feeling disconnected from your body), derealization (feeling disconnected from reality), dissociative amnesia (losing gaps of time), somatoform dissociation (physical pain with no medical explanation), or structural dissociation (often referred to as personality disorders).

## HOW DOES DISSOCIATION AFFECT EMDR THERAPY?

The important thing to understand is that at one time, dissociation was really helpful. It was a way for the individual to survive a very uncomfortable or threatening experience; however, it can be much less helpful when we're trying to reprocess a traumatic event in counseling. The more you try to think about something (PTSD is a lack of time orientation), the more the dissociation is going to still try to jump in to try to protect you. So before reprocessing anything in phase 4, you first have to increase your sense of safety and ability to stay partially present. This is the concept of dual awareness: to have one foot in the past and one foot in the present. This is how traumatic experiences are effectively reprocessed without re-traumatization.

It's helpful for many individuals with a history of trauma to assess their levels of dissociation prior to doing trauma work. This can be done with the DESI-II (Dissociative Experiences Scale) as a way to measure dissociation. The higher your score, the more preparation work (phase 2) you'll need before proceeding to the reprocessing phases of EMDR Therapy.

## HOW DO YOU DECREASE DISSOCIATION LEVELS?

It's important to understand how dissociation can impact the ability to overcome a trauma. More often than not, individuals who do have levels of dissociation report feeling stuck. It's the difference between knowing a trauma is over, but still not able to actually feel better or achieve your therapy goals.

# TRAUMA & DISSOCIATION

It's very important for both clients and clinicians to understand the dissociative model when working through any type of trauma.

This is why Preparation (Phase 2 of EMDR) is so important. Mindfulness skills are some of the best ways to decrease dissociation. Since dissociation is the lack of being present, and mindfulness is the act of being present, it would stand to reason that mindfulness is the antidote for dissociation.

By strengthening your ability to be present, your window of tolerance expands, and thus, so does your ability to tolerate uncomfortable aspects of the trauma reprocessing work.

In cases of Structural Dissociation, your therapist may introduce *Parts Work* or *Ego State Therapy* during the Preparation Phase. This is a helpful way to become more aware of your different parts, which helps you be able to reprocess traumatic experiences.

The topic of parts and ego states is fascinating, and more than we can go into in this book, but there are several books (*see Recommended Readings*) that go into more detail about this and are very helpful for those struggling with complex trauma.

Building self awareness of your own inner experiences and becoming aware of the felt sense is a crucial element of trauma recovery. The next chapter will go into more detail about the nervous system and give information to help you increase your awareness of your own sense of self.

"The essence of trauma is disconnection from ourselves. Trauma is not terrible things that happen from the other side—those are traumatic. But the trauma is the very separation from the body and emotions."

- *Gabor Maté*

# Building Self Awareness

# UNDERSTANDING YOUR NERVOUS SYSTEM

Understanding the nervous system is an invaluable part of the trauma healing process. Read on to learn more about the nervous system, how it can be affected by experiences, and how to rewire your nervous system and prepare for trauma reprocessing.

# *Building Self Awareness*
# THE NERVOUS SYSTEM

Understanding how your nervous system works and responds to stressors can be very helpful for survivors of trauma. Many times, individuals will learn about how trauma affects the stress response system in the body and say, "so I'm not crazy?" No, you're not! Your nervous system developed in response to your environment. There's nothing wrong with you. *It's science.*

Research from Dr. Stephen Porges and Deb Dana on *Polyvagal Theory* has helped us to understand what happens to us biologically when we experience a stressful event(s). Their research involves focusing on the Vagus Nerve, which plays a crucial role in the functioning of our autonomic nervous system. *(See Recommended Readings to learn more about this... it's fascinating stuff!)*

## WHAT IS OUR AUTONOMIC NERVOUS SYSTEM?
The autonomic nervous system (ANS) controls all the involuntary functions in the body, including: heart rate, breathing, digestion, sexual arousal, and all those functions that happen inside the body, without having to give it conscious thought.

The ANS is broken down into two main parts: The sympathetic nervous system (SNS) and the parasympathetic nervous system (PNS). The PNS then branches into two parts: the ventral vagal and the dorsal vagal. *(See image below)*

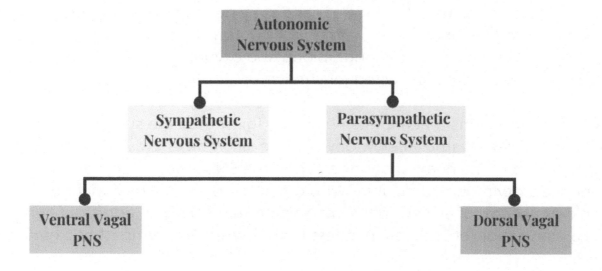

# THE NERVOUS SYSTEM

The SNS is commonly known as hyperarousal, or "fight or flight". A sensitized SNS typically shows up as anxiety, panic attacks, avoidance and anger. The ventral vagal branch of the PNS, commonly known as "rest and digest", is when we are calm and connected. The dorsal vagal branch of the PNS, commonly known as hypoarousal, is another mode of survival and can manifest as chronic depression and dissociation.

It's important to note that individuals who are stuck in SNS or Dorsal Vagal PNS activation may often struggle in their interpersonal relationships. This is because the social engagement system (ventral vagal PNS) is offline, so we are less likely to be able to connect with others when we are in a state of protection. Let's break each state down in more detail.

### THE VENTRAL VAGAL PARASYMPATHETIC NERVOUS SYSTEM

The ventral vagal PNS is our social engagement system and is activated when we feel safe and our brains do not detect any danger or threats to our survival. This allows us to socially connect with others, be playful, think clearly, sleep well, and allows the body to engage in restorative functions for better health.

### THE SYMPATHETIC NERVOUS SYSTEM

When our brains detect danger, our SNS automatically kicks in. The function of the SNS is to mobilize us in the face of danger by directing all of our energy to our body's primitive functions for immediate survival. Our heart rate and breathing increase so we get enough blood and oxygen to the body to fight back or escape. We are hard-wired for survival.

Other bodily functions that are less necessary for immediate survival, such as digestion and sexual arousal, slow down, since all of the energy in the body is being diverted to the heart and lungs. When the SNS is activated, you may experience a dry mouth, difficulties with digestion, or sexual dysfunction. Chronic symptoms of anxiety, panic attacks, anger, feeling on edge, difficulty with concentration, etc. can all manifest from a sensitized sympathetic nervous system.

# THE NERVOUS SYSTEM

**THE DORSAL VAGAL PARASYMPATHETIC NERVOUS SYSTEM**

If we perceive danger in an escapable situation, the dorsal vagal PNS kicks in. The purpose of the this branch of the PNS is to *immobilize and dissociate.* Doing so helps the conscious mind go offline so we don't have to experience pain and can conserve energy if a chance to escape or fight back arises.

When the dorsal vagal PNS is activated, a range of symptoms may occur, including: slower heart rate, fatigue, feeling disconnected from the body (depersonalization) or environment (derealization), fainting, or feeling frozen, numb, and/or lightheaded.

Chronic symptoms of depression, memory loss, dissociation, chronic fatigue and unexplained physical pain may all be manifestations of a nervous system that is stuck in dorsal vagal shutdown.

If you have a nervous system that has been stuck in dorsal vagal shutdown for a while, it's important to work on rewiring your nervous system slowly and gently. As you work your way out of dorsal vagal, you may go through SNS before reaching ventral vagal.

*Think of it like this...*

If dorsal vagal is the bottom rung of a ladder, and ventral vagal is the top part of the ladder, you have to move through the SNS, which is the middle part of the ladder. So experiences of anxiety, discomfort or other types of mobilizing activation are common during the process. Just know that this is short term and is a sign that what you're doing is working as you are work your way up to feeling calm and connected.

The graphic on the following page helps to depict this concept in greater detail.

Remember as the saying goes, *you have to feel it to heal it!*

# THE NERVOUS SYSTEM

## *The Autonomic Ladder*

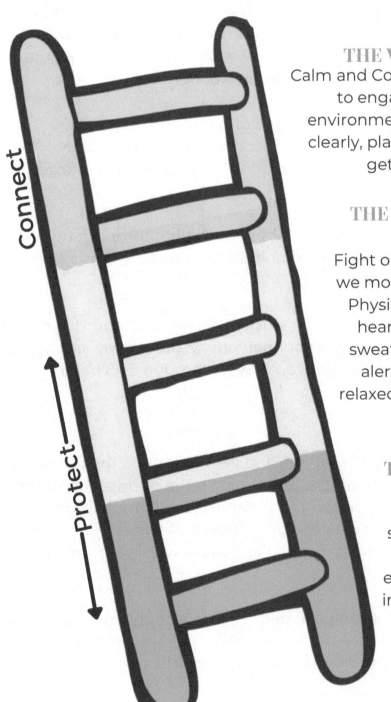

### THE VENTRAL VAGAL PNS

Calm and Connected. We feel safe and able to engage and interact with our environment. We're able to focus, think clearly, plan and tolerate stress without getting highjacked by it.

### THE SYMPATHETIC NERVOUS SYSTEM

Fight or Flight. We perceive danger so we mobilize as an attempt at survival. Physical symptoms include: racing heart, anxiety, dry mouth, anger, sweating, dilated pupils, increased alertness, increased respiration, relaxed bladder and slowing down of digestion

### THE DORSAL VAGAL PNS

Freeze. Perceived danger seems inescapable, so we shutdown and dissociate from ourselves and/or our environment and escape to our inner world. Physical symptoms include: feeling faint, numb, lightheaded, depressed, fatigued, memory loss, and zoning out.

# Building Self Awareness
# THE NERVOUS SYSTEM

## HOW TRAUMA AFFECTS THE NERVOUS SYSTEM

Trauma can have a strong impact on the autonomic nervous system and impair its ability to work correctly. Experiencing trauma can cause the nervous system to *perceive* danger, even when there may not actually be any danger present. This faulty perception is when something triggers you, even without your knowledge, and effects how you think, feel and act. Your conscious mind knows there is no danger present, but your body starts to act like there is, before your conscious mind has a chance to even notice what's happening. All of a sudden you may start feeling anxious, depressed, have a racing heart or difficulty breathing, and have no idea why. This is the difference between reacting and thoughtfully responding.

### *Think of it like this...*

Imagine a home has an alarm system (our body's sympathetic nervous system), and because of certain things happening in the home (like break-ins, broken windows, etc.) the alarm system has become more sensitized. So now, the wind blows, and the alarm system thinks there is danger present and starts going off, even though there is no actual danger. The alarm system just *thinks, feels and acts* like there is. If that alarm system goes off for too long without being shut off, it may eventually burn out or shut down (which is the dorsal vagal PNS kicking in.)

This is exactly how trauma can impact how our nervous system perceives our environment. Because of something(s) that happened in the past, our nervous system can become overly sensitized and perceive danger, even when there is no actual danger present.

## THE WINDOW OF TOLERANCE

The window of tolerance is another way to describe the nervous system. The window of tolerance is the optimal zone of arousal in which a person can function effectively. Basically, it means that you can feel stressed, but still function and not be highjacked by your emotions. Stressful life experiences can often make your window of tolerance really small, making it difficult to stay balanced or present when stressed.

# THE NERVOUS SYSTEM

Going above the window of tolerance is when the SNS is activated, and going below is when the dorsal vagal PNS is activated.

Phase 2 of EMDR helps widen the window of tolerance so that you can process distressing experiences while still staying within the edges of the window of tolerance. This helps you process thoughts, emotions and sensations related to traumatic experiences without shutting down or going into an intolerable panic.

## REWIRING YOUR NERVOUS SYSTEM

Resourcing and stabilization exercises in phase 2 of EMDR help to decrease the activation of the SNS and increase the activity of the ventral vagal PNS. One of the benefits of EMDR Therapy as a whole is that it helps to rewire your nervous system from these exercises, as well as from the reprocessing of traumatic experiences.

In addition to EMDR Therapy, there are other ways to support the rewiring of the nervous system and improve the tone of the vagus nerve. Some of these ways include: deep breathing, meditation, biofeedback, humming, contrast showers (alternating hot and cold), proper nutrition and exercise, laughter, singing and dancing, yoga and massage therapy.

Engaging in these types of activities can really support your progress with EMDR and possibly even help you reach your treatment goals faster.

*It's important to consult with your therapist and physician before engaging in any new regimen to ensure your health and safety.*

# Building Self Awareness
# YOUR NERVOUS SYSTEM
## *Common Types of Trauma Responses*

Below is a brief overview of common types of responses to distress. Take a look and see which may feel familiar to you. Your responses may vary depending on the trigger or your current functioning level. Everyone's nervous system is uniquely different and can change with time and circumstances.

| RESPONSE | ACTIVATION TYPE | PRESENTATION | MORE INFO |
|---|---|---|---|
| **FIGHT** | Sympathetic Nervous system / Hyperarousal | Angry outbursts, chronic defensiveness, combative & argumentative | Fighting back when danger is present to keep yourself safe |
| **FLIGHT** | Sympathetic nervous system / Hyperarousal | Avoidance, canceling plans all the time, social anxiety | Running away to avoid a dangerous situation |
| **ATTACHMENT CRY** | Sympathetic Nervous System / Hyperarousal | Difficulty with being alone. Looking to others to help regulate your emotions, reverting to state of child-like dependency, feeling unsafe when others do not respond to you. | Often referred to as "borderline personality disorder" What infants do when they need a caretaker to respond to them, since infants are helpless and need to be taken care of. When an attachment cry is not consistently responded to, that child learns to believe on a subconscious level that "I will not survive unless you take care of me." |
| **FAWN** | Sympathetic Nervous System / Hyperarousal | People pleasing. Consistently putting the needs of others before yourself. | Often a subconscious way to keep yourself safe. "If I keep you happy, I will be safe." |
| **FRIGHT** | Blended states of hyper + hypoarousal. Shifts between SNS + Dorsal Vagal PNS. | Panic attacks, dizziness, lightheadedness | Occurs when we cannot escape. Signs of dissociation may begin to show |
| **FREEZE** | Dorsal Vagal PNS / Hypoarousal | Difficulty making decisions, never sure how you feel, feeling stuck, "deer caught in the headlights" | Occurs briefly before activation occurs. Scanning the environment for danger, social referencing (looking at how others respond to determine how you respond) |
| **FAINT** | Dorsal Vagal PNS / Hypoarousal | Body drops to the ground, possible loss of consciousness. Often called a vasovagal reaction. | Your body's attempt at keeping blood flow to your brain |
| **COLLAPSE** | Dorsal Vagal PNS / Hypoarousal | Dissociation dominates. May feel like nothing can help you, shutdown, numb. May have chronic pain with no medical explanation. | Common in chronic traumatization, when you could not fight back/run away. Often called treatment resistant depression. |

# Building Self Awareness
## SELF REFLECTION

Now that you know more about nervous system responses, what have you noticed about yourself and how your own nervous system reacts to your environment?

# *Building Self Awareness*
# SELF REFLECTION
## ...continued...

# Building Self Awareness
## SELF REFLECTION
### ...continued...

*Part Two*

# ALL ABOUT YOU

Now you know all there is to know about the EMDR Therapy process, so let's get to work! This section is all about YOU. The following writing prompts, checklists, and logs are designed to get you thinking, improve your clarity, and help you monitor your own progress throughout EMDR Therapy.

*Phase 1*

# HISTORY TAKING & TREATMENT PLANNING

# *My story*
# THIS
# IS ME

(Your Name Here)

_____

"The past impacts our present without our even being aware of it."

- *Francine Shapiro*

**founder of EMDR therapy**

## *My struggle*

The current issue(s) I am struggling with and am seeking EMDR Therapy for is:

_____

_____

_____

_____

## *My outcomes*

The outcome I am hoping to achieve with EMDR Therapy is:

_____

_____

_____

_____

# What's Your Why?

Everyone has their own reasons for why they want to pursue therapy. Writing about the driving forces behind your decision to start trauma treatment can be a helpful and inspiring part of the process.

Revisit this section as often as you need to to remind yourself of your why if you feel discouraged, overwhelmed, or want to add more!

## My why

My motivation for getting EMDR Therapy includes:

_____

_____

_____

_____

_____

_____

# *Symptom*
# CHECKLIST

Getting a list of your present day symptoms is a helpful way to bridge back to the past experiences where they started. The more information you share with your therapist, the better. Therapy is a judgement free zone! An honest, comprehensive history helps your therapist to best help you!

**Some of the symptoms I struggle with (past/present) include: (check all that apply)**

☐ Flashbacks          ☐ Chronic pain          ☐ Disordered eating          ☐ Generalized anxiety

☐ Panic attacks          ☐ Derealization          ☐ Depression          ☐ Angry outbursts

☐ Avoidance          ☐ Feeling out of body          ☐ Feeling numb          ☐ Thoughts of suicide

☐ Self-harm          ☐ People pleasing          ☐ Substance abuse          ☐ Social isolation

☐ Alcohol abuse          ☐ Difficulty managing relationships          ☐ Intrusive thoughts          ☐ Unable to control my emotions

☐ Losing gaps of time          ☐ Memory Loss

☐ Other addictive behaviors (describe) _____
_____

Additional symptoms:
_____
_____

Previous diagnoses I have been given in the past include: (if applicable)
_____
_____

Other information that is important for my therapist to know:
_____
_____

*Treatment Goals*

# I WANT LESS...

What are the current thoughts, emotions, behaviors and sensations you am currently struggling with and WANT LESS of after completing EMDR Therapy?

## Thoughts

Thoughts I want to
have LESS of are:

_____

_____

_____

_____

_____

## Emotions

Emotions I want to feel LESS
of/more in control of are:

_____

_____

_____

_____

_____

## Behaviors

Behaviors I want to
do LESS of include:

_____

_____

_____

_____

_____

## Sensations

Sensations in my body I want
to experience LESS of are:

_____

_____

_____

_____

_____

# Treatment Goals
# I WANT MORE...

What are the thoughts, emotions, behaviors and sensations you want to experience MORE OF/MORE FULLY through EMDR Therapy?

## Thoughts

Thoughts I want to have MORE of are:

_____

_____

_____

_____

_____

## Emotions

Emotions I want to feel MORE of/more in control of are:

_____

_____

_____

_____

_____

## Behaviors

Behaviors I want to do MORE of include:

_____

_____

_____

_____

_____

## Sensations

Sensations in my body I want to experience MORE of are:

_____

_____

_____

_____

_____

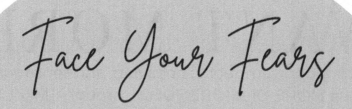

# Face Your Fears

It is very common to have concerns or fears when starting any healing journey. It's important to acknowledge those concerns head on and bring them up with your therapist so you can explore them together.

Facing your fears directly will help to uncover possible barriers to treatment and increase your feelings of safety throughout the process.

## My concerns

My concerns about the EMDR Process are:

_____

_____

_____

_____

_____

_____

# TRIGGERS & MEMORIES

## LINKING THE PRESENT TO THE PAST

Triggers are doorways to our past experiences that need healing. Phase 1 of EMDR includes increasing your awareness of what your triggers are and linking them to the experiences where those emotional responses began.

We experience triggers in our day to day life and they activate our nervous system, without us giving conscious thought to it, and cause present day symptoms, such as anxiety, flashbacks, behavioral outbursts and more. Triggers can be *anything*, including a smell, a sound, times of year, a thought, a person, or anything that has the smallest thread of association to something from the past.

Making a list of your triggers helps to increase your awareness of your own nervous system, as well as provide valuable information in creating your treatment plan in EMDR Therapy.

It's not uncommon to be unsure of what your triggers are, since the nervous system can respond so quickly, faster than conscious thought. Mindfulness practices, some as breathing exercises and guided meditation, help to slow your thinking down and bring insight into what happens right before you get activated. Your therapist is there to help guide you and support you if you get stuck figuring it out.

It's important to note that emotional neglect is common in survivors of complex trauma, so you can also write down time periods of the memories you do *not* have. For example, where there times were you needed more support/validation/acknowledgement and you were not able to get it? Make note of those time periods above.

During treatment planning, it may be helpful to narrow down the FIRST, WORST, and MOST RECENT experiences in regards to a specific theme that you are working on with your therapist. This helps to find an "entryway" into a memory network so that you can begin to reprocess those experiences during phase 4 of EMDR.

# *Phase 1*
# LIST OF TRIGGERS

Directions: Use the chart below to make a list of the triggers you have identified (column on the left), how you respond when you are triggered (middle column), and the way that you want to be able to respond to that trigger in the future (column on the right).

| TRIGGER | TRAUMA/NERVOUS SYSTEM RESPONSE | FUTURE DESIRED OUTCOME |
|---|---|---|
| | | |
| | | |
| | | |
| | | |
| | | |
| | | |
| | | |
| | | |
| | | |
| | | |
| | | |
| | | |
| | | |
| | | |
| | | |
| | | |
| | | |
| | | |
| | | |
| | | |

# *Phase 1*
# LIST OF TRIGGERS

Directions: Use the chart below to make a list of the triggers you have identified (column on the left), how you respond when you are triggered (middle column), and the way that you want to be able to respond to that trigger in the future (column on the right).

| TRIGGER | TRAUMA/NERVOUS SYSTEM RESPONSE | FUTURE DESIRED OUTCOME |
|---|---|---|
|  |  |  |
|  |  |  |
|  |  |  |
|  |  |  |
|  |  |  |
|  |  |  |
|  |  |  |
|  |  |  |
|  |  |  |
|  |  |  |
|  |  |  |
|  |  |  |
|  |  |  |
|  |  |  |
|  |  |  |
|  |  |  |
|  |  |  |
|  |  |  |
|  |  |  |
|  |  |  |

# LIST OF TRIGGERS

Directions: Use the chart below to make a list of the triggers you have identified (column on the left), how you respond when you are triggered (middle column), and the way that you want to be able to respond to that trigger in the future (column on the right).

| TRIGGER | TRAUMA/NERVOUS SYSTEM RESPONSE | FUTURE DESIRED OUTCOME |
|---|---|---|
| | | |

*Phase 1*

# LIST OF TRIGGERS

Directions: Use the chart below to make a list of the triggers you have identified (column on the left), how you respond when you are triggered (middle column), and the way that you want to be able to respond to that trigger in the future (column on the right).

| TRIGGER | TRAUMA/NERVOUS SYSTEM RESPONSE | FUTURE DESIRED OUTCOME |
|---------|-------------------------------|------------------------|
|         |                               |                        |
|         |                               |                        |
|         |                               |                        |
|         |                               |                        |
|         |                               |                        |
|         |                               |                        |
|         |                               |                        |
|         |                               |                        |
|         |                               |                        |
|         |                               |                        |
|         |                               |                        |
|         |                               |                        |
|         |                               |                        |
|         |                               |                        |
|         |                               |                        |
|         |                               |                        |
|         |                               |                        |
|         |                               |                        |
|         |                               |                        |
|         |                               |                        |

# LIST OF MEMORIES

Directions: Now that you have identified what your triggers are, it's time to link them to the experiences they are connected to. Use the columns below to list the trigger (left), what the triggers reminds you of (middle), and the age or time period when that original experience took place.

| TRIGGER | WHAT THE TRIGGER REMINDS YOU OF | AGE/TIME PERIOD |
|---|---|---|
| | | |
| | | |
| | | |
| | | |
| | | |
| | | |
| | | |
| | | |
| | | |
| | | |
| | | |
| | | |
| | | |
| | | |
| | | |
| | | |

# LIST OF MEMORIES

Directions: Now that you have identified what your triggers are, it's time to link them to the experiences they are connected to. Use the columns below to list the trigger (left), what the triggers reminds you of (middle), and the age or time period when that original experience took place.

| TRIGGER | WHAT THE TRIGGER REMINDS YOU OF | AGE/TIME PERIOD |
|---|---|---|
|  |  |  |
|  |  |  |
|  |  |  |
|  |  |  |
|  |  |  |
|  |  |  |
|  |  |  |
|  |  |  |
|  |  |  |
|  |  |  |
|  |  |  |
|  |  |  |
|  |  |  |
|  |  |  |
|  |  |  |
|  |  |  |

# LIST OF MEMORIES

Directions: Now that you have identified what your triggers are, it's time to link them to the experiences they are connected to. Use the columns below to list the trigger (left), what the triggers reminds you of (middle), and the age or time period when that original experience took place.

| TRIGGER | WHAT THE TRIGGER REMINDS YOU OF | AGE/TIME PERIOD |
|---------|--------------------------------|-----------------|
|         |                                |                 |
|         |                                |                 |
|         |                                |                 |
|         |                                |                 |
|         |                                |                 |
|         |                                |                 |
|         |                                |                 |
|         |                                |                 |
|         |                                |                 |
|         |                                |                 |
|         |                                |                 |
|         |                                |                 |
|         |                                |                 |
|         |                                |                 |
|         |                                |                 |
|         |                                |                 |
|         |                                |                 |
|         |                                |                 |
|         |                                |                 |

# LIST OF MEMORIES

Directions: Now that you have identified what your triggers are, it's time to link them to the experiences they are connected to. Use the columns below to list the trigger (left), what the triggers reminds you of (middle), and the age or time period when that original experience took place.

| TRIGGER | WHAT THE TRIGGER REMINDS YOU OF | AGE/TIME PERIOD |
|---|---|---|
| | | |
| | | |
| | | |
| | | |
| | | |
| | | |
| | | |
| | | |
| | | |
| | | |
| | | |
| | | |
| | | |
| | | |
| | | |
| | | |
| | | |
| | | |
| | | |
| | | |

*Preparation*

# BUILDING READINESS FOR REPROCESSING

# WHY IT'S IMPORTANT

Phase 2 of EMDR, known as the Preparation Stage, is a vital part of EMDR Therapy. The purpose is to create a safety net before working on distressing memories and emotions, and to promote dual awareness (the ability to have one foot in a past memory and one foot in the present moment.) This phase focuses on creating and enhancing tools and skills to practice in between sessions to improve your readiness for trauma processing. While preparation is Phase 2 of EMDR Therapy, it can be done at any time whenever you identify the need for a new resource.

### *Think of it like this...*

Imagine meeting a swim instructor for the first time. A good instructor would make sure you know how to swim before throwing you in the deep end of the pool.  First, they would find out what supports you already have (like swimmies or a life preserver, and make sure you have access to them before getting in). They would assess what skills you need to learn to be able to swim successfully.

# TWO TYPES OF RESOURCES

**1**

**Existing resources that you need greater access to**

Think of it like looking for a life preserver you already have and ensuring you know where it is before you get in the pool.

Some examples may include: identifying existing supportive people, enhancing strengths you already have or increasing your ability access to them, improving emotion regulation skills.

**2**

**Resources that need to be created to be able to handle reprocessing**

Think of it like learning the mechanics of how to swim before getting in the deep end.

Some examples may include: teaching emotion regulation skills, identifying and installing attachment figures, containment exercises, creating a calm place, and learning how to access the felt sense in the body.

# PRACTICE = PROGRESS

It's important to practice these skills on a regular basis, especially in between sessions with your therapist. The more you practice, the faster you'll make progress toward your treatment goals. Going back to the swimming analogy, the instructor can teach you the mechanics to learn how to swim, but if you don't practice regularly on your own, it will take that much longer to learn.

Once the reprocessing phases start, you may notice an initial increase in discomfort, so it's helpful to review this your list of resources frequently so you can readily access these tools if discomfort arises.

Remember that if something does not work immediately, it does not mean that it won't work. It takes *Time, Repetition, Patience & Understanding* when learning a new skill. So practice and be patient with yourself while you are learning.

The following are some exercises that you may use during the preparation stage, but they are only a suggestion out of many other possibilities.

The *most important* thing to remember is to choose the resources that work for YOU! Your therapist will help you find what works best for you.

*My thoughts regarding preparation...*

# THE CONTAINER

The container is an exercise that is intended to help you regulate disturbance, improve focus and help you function in the face of distress. Your container may be used in between sessions or during processing to create a felt sense of safety. You can also create multiple containers if you find that useful.

**Directions**: Imagine a container that it big enough, strong enough and fully secure, so that it can hold any upsetting images, memories, sounds, smells, sensations, thoughts or emotions.  Include as many details as possible so it feels secure. You can also create multiple containers. *Be sure that this container does not have any negative associations to it so that that it maintains a feeling of safety.*

What material is it made out of it so it is secure? What shape is it? Does it have a texture? How heavy is it? What color(s) is it? How do you secure it? (Lock, bolt, etc.) Any other defining characteristics about it?

Now, think of something mildly irritating. Notice how you feel as you bring that irritating concept to mind. Open your container and put it in there, taking as long as you need to make sure it is in there securely.  Close and lock the container and visualize yourself walking away.  As you do so, notice how you feel as you get further and further away from the container.

Practice using your container regularly between sessions.  The more you practice using it, the better it works!

Communicate any difficulties you may have with this exercise with your therapist, who can help you navigate those challenges.  Again, not every resource works the same for everyone. If this does not resonate with you, no worries! Your therapist is there to find the resources that work best for you!

*Preparation*

# THE CONTAINER

Use the space below to describe the details of your container. You can also
draw your container or attach a picture of it.

# CALM/PEACEFUL PLACE

The goal of this exercise is to help increase your ability to access a positive feeling state and learn how to shift the state of your nervous system (moving from stressed to calm.)

**Directions:** Imagine a place, real or imagined, that you associate with feelings of being calm and peaceful. As you imagine it, describe all that you see, including images, objects, colors, etc. Are there any scents that you can smell in this place? What sounds do you hear? As you imagine this place, what emotions are you feeling? What sensations do you feel in your body as you feel that feeling? Describe with as much detail as you'd like to help bring this place to life.

Once you have a sense of calm or peacefulness as you imagine this space, begin to tap it in slowly, alternating left and right forms of BLS, 6-12 times.

What word or phrase comes to mind as you are experiencing this positive feeling state? _____

Repeat this phrase again as you tap again and feel this positive feeling state. Then, practice saying this word/phrase again and noticing how you feel when you say it (without tapping). *This helps to pair the word/phrase with the positive state you are currently experiencing.*

Now, think of something slightly irritating. As you focus on that annoyance, notice what you feel emotionally and in your body. Bring your attention back to your calm place while saying your cue word to yourself. Pause and notice your feeling state as it shifts. Once you access the calm/peaceful feeling again, tap yourself slowly again 6-12 times.

You can continue this practice of noticing the disturbance and shifting back to calm as much as you'd like, while tapping in the positive experience each time you're able to shift.

Practice using your calm place and cue words in between sessions.

*Preparation*

# CALM/PEACEFUL PLACE

Use the space below to describe your calm place. You can also draw or attach a picture of your calm/peaceful place.

# THE REMOTE CONTROL

The Emotional Remote is a helpful resource to reduce the intensity of emotions and reactions during processing, as well as in between sessions. This resource is an empowerment tool to help you feel more in control over your emotions and how they affect you.

**Directions**: Bring to mind an image of a remote control that you can use when the intensity of emotions feels overwhelming. This remote has all the buttons and features needed to help you regulate your inner experience. You can use it to change the channel, reduce or increase the volume, pause, rewind, fast forward, change the colors, etc.

What color is the remote? What size is it? What type of buttons does it have? Imagine the feeling of the weight of this remote in your hand and what the texture of this remote feels like.

Now, bring to mind a recent experience that was slightly irritating to practice using this remote. As that concept comes to mind, notice what emotions and sensations you are experiencing. Imagine using this remote to modulate the experience you feeling right now. You can tone down the intensity, change the channel, or anything else you need to help you

Once you start to feel the sense of control over your experience, slowly tap in this sense of control using a slow form of BLS for about 6-12 passes.

You can also use other visualizations, such as a dimmer switch, radio knobs, a thermostat or anything that has an adjustable quality to it.

Practice using this resource in between sessions whenever you feel a sense of overwhelm or not in control of your own inner experience.

This resource can also be used during reprocessing whenever the intensity of the experience is overwhelming, or if dissociation is creeping in (hypoarousal) and you want to increase the intensity so you can be activated enough to continue reprocessing.

# THE REMOTE CONTROL

Use the space below to describe your emotional remote. You can also draw or attach a picture of the remote control.

# ATTACHMENT FIGURES

*Attachment Focused EMDR* (Laurel Parnell) is a fantastic approach when working through relational and attachment trauma. In the space below, make a list of real or imaginary figures who possess nurturing, protective and wise qualities, as well as real or imaginary figures who would be your ideal parent.caregiver. Once you feel a sense of those qualities, tap them in using slow BLS.

### Nurturing Figures

_____
_____
_____
_____
_____
_____

### Protective Figures

_____
_____
_____
_____
_____
_____

### Wise Figures

_____
_____
_____
_____
_____
_____

### Ideal Parents/Caregivers

_____
_____
_____
_____
_____
_____

*Note: This may be activating for some individuals who never felt cared for or protected, which is why it is important to do this with the help of a therapist.*

# MY RESOURCES

Directions: Use this list as a summary of all your resources so you have a convenient place to easily refer back to as needed throughout treatment.

| RESOURCE NAME | DETAILS | HOW IT HELPS ME |
|---|---|---|
|  |  |  |
|  |  |  |
|  |  |  |
|  |  |  |
|  |  |  |
|  |  |  |
|  |  |  |
|  |  |  |
|  |  |  |
|  |  |  |
|  |  |  |
|  |  |  |
|  |  |  |

*Note*

Update this list as often as you need to and review it frequently to keep these resources at the forefront of your mind.

*Preparation*
# MY RESOURCES

Directions: Use this list as a summary of all your resources so you have a convenient place to easily refer back to as needed throughout treatment.

| RESOURCE NAME | DETAILS | HOW IT HELPS ME |
|---|---|---|
| | | |
| | | |
| | | |
| | | |
| | | |
| | | |
| | | |
| | | |
| | | |
| | | |
| | | |
| | | |
| | | |
| | | |

*Note*

Update this list as often as you need to and review it frequently to keep these resources at the forefront of your mind.

# MY RESOURCES

Directions: Use this list as a summary of all your resources so you have a convenient place to easily refer back to as needed throughout treatment.

| RESOURCE NAME | DETAILS | HOW IT HELPS ME |
| --- | --- | --- |
| | | |
| | | |
| | | |
| | | |
| | | |
| | | |
| | | |
| | | |
| | | |
| | | |
| | | |
| | | |
| | | |
| | | |

*Note*

Update this list as often as you need to and review it frequently to keep these resources at the forefront of your mind.

# MY RESOURCES

Directions: Use this list as a summary of all your resources so you have a convenient place to easily refer back to as needed throughout treatment.

| RESOURCE NAME | DETAILS | HOW IT HELPS ME |
| --- | --- | --- |
| | | |
| | | |
| | | |
| | | |
| | | |
| | | |
| | | |
| | | |
| | | |
| | | |
| | | |
| | | |

*Note*

Update this list as often as you need to and review it frequently to keep these resources at the forefront of your mind.

# MY RESOURCES

Directions: Use this list as a summary of all your resources so you have a convenient place to easily refer back to as needed throughout treatment.

| RESOURCE NAME | DETAILS | HOW IT HELPS ME |
|---|---|---|
| | | |
| | | |
| | | |
| | | |
| | | |
| | | |
| | | |
| | | |
| | | |
| | | |
| | | |
| | | |
| | | |
| | | |

*Note*

Update this list as often as you need to and review it frequently to keep these resources at the forefront of your mind.

*Phase 4*

# REPROCESSING

This section will support you through the reprocessing phases of EMDR.  Included is a breakdown of what to expect, as well as reflection sheets and logs to use in-between reprocessing sessions.

# *Reprocessing*
# WHAT TO EXPECT

Ever hear that saying, "It Gets Worse Before It Gets Better?"
Well, that's kind of the case with EMDR Therapy, too.

Once you start phase 4, the part where you begin reprocessing past
traumatic experiences and doing the eye movements/tapping/audio tones,
it's not uncommon to experience the following:

✓ Increase in dreaming/nightmares
✓ Difficulty sleeping
✓ More on edge than usual
✓ Increased levels of anxiety

It's important to remember that **this is short term.**

## *Think of it like this...*

Imagine shaking a soda bottle up and unscrewing the top. The soda explodes
everywhere at first, and then it settles down and the soda goes back to a non-
explosive state. And after all that carbonation gets out, it's much less likely to
explode again because all the carbonation was released. So even if you shake
the bottle again, it won't have the same explosive reaction because all of the
carbonated energy has been released.

This is exactly what the reprocessing stages of EMDR do. They shake up the
brain and the nervous system by bringing all your attention to experiences that
have not been fully addressed. Doing so helps the thoughts, emotions and
sensations related to experience(s) to finally release.

When you begin working on a traumatic experience, you may feel varying levels
of discomfort, just like the soda fizzing everywhere. During this time, refer to
the tools you established during phase 2 (resourcing) to support you. It's also
important to make note of these things in between sessions, which is why
keeping a log in between sessions can help you with your progress. As long as
you stay the course, you will start to see an improvement as all the traumatic
material gets cleared out.

*Reprocessing*

# SESSION SUMMARY

Use this form after each reprocessing session to help increase your self awareness and support your progress. You can also use the TICES log to keep track of how you feel in between sessions.

Today's Date: _____     Theme/Experience I worked on today:

Time Period I'm working on:

☐ Past

☐ Present

☐ Future

### How do you feel after today's session?

### Was anything challenging/difficult about today's session?

### Resources that can help me in between sessions?

*Notes*

### Other insights from today?

# *Reprocessing*
# SESSION SUMMARY

Use this form after each reprocessing session to help increase your self awareness and support your progress. You can also use the TICES log to keep track of how you feel in between sessions.

Today's Date: _____

Theme/Experience I worked on today:

Time Period I'm working on:

☐ Past

☐ Present

☐ Future

_____

_____

_____

_____

### How do you feel after today's session?

_____

_____

### Was anything challenging/difficult about today's session?

_____

_____

### Resources that can help me in between sessions?

_____

_____

## *Notes*

### Other insights from today?

_____

_____

*Reprocessing*

# SESSION SUMMARY

Use this form after each reprocessing session to help increase your self awareness and support your progress. You can also use the TICES log to keep track of how you feel in between sessions.

Today's Date: _____

Time Period I'm working on:

☐ Past

☐ Present

☐ Future

Theme/Experience I worked on today:

_____

_____

_____

_____

### How do you feel after today's session?

_____

_____

### Was anything challenging/difficult about today's session?

_____

_____

### Resources that can help me in between sessions?

_____

_____

*Notes*

### Other insights from today?

_____

_____

# *Reprocessing*
# SESSION SUMMARY

Use this form after each reprocessing session to help increase your self awareness and support your progress. You can also use the TICES log to keep track of how you feel in between sessions.

Today's Date: _____

Time Period I'm working on:

☐ Past

☐ Present

☐ Future

Theme/Experience I worked on today:

_____

_____

_____

_____

### How do you feel after today's session?

_____

_____

### Was anything challenging/difficult about today's session?

_____

_____

### Resources that can help me in between sessions?

_____

_____

## *Notes*

### Other insights from today?

_____

_____

*Reprocessing*
# SESSION SUMMARY

Use this form after each reprocessing session to help increase your self awareness and support your progress. You can also use the TICES log to keep track of how you feel in between sessions.

Today's Date: _____     Theme/Experience I worked on today:

Time Period I'm working on:

☐ Past

☐ Present

☐ Future

### How do you feel after today's session?

_____

_____

### Was anything challenging/difficult about today's session?

_____

_____

### Resources that can help me in between sessions?

_____

_____

*Notes*

### Other insights from today?

_____

_____

# *Reprocessing*
# SESSION SUMMARY

Use this form after each reprocessing session to help increase your self awareness and support your progress. You can also use the TICES log to keep track of how you feel in between sessions.

Today's Date: _____       Theme/Experience I worked on today:

Time Period I'm working on:       _____

☐ Past                            _____

☐ Present                         _____

☐ Future                          _____

### How do you feel after today's session?

_____

_____

### Was anything challenging/difficult about today's session?

_____

_____

### Resources that can help me in between sessions?

_____

_____

## *Notes*

Other insights from today?

_____

_____

*Reprocessing*

# SESSION SUMMARY

Use this form after each reprocessing session to help increase your self awareness and support your progress. You can also use the TICES log to keep track of how you feel in between sessions.

Today's Date: _____

Time Period I'm working on:

☐ Past

☐ Present

☐ Future

Theme/Experience I worked on today:

_____

_____

_____

_____

How do you feel after today's session?

_____

_____

Was anything challenging/difficult about today's session?

_____

_____

Resources that can help me in between sessions?

_____

_____

*Notes*

Other insights from today?

_____

_____

# *Reprocessing*
# SESSION SUMMARY

Use this form after each reprocessing session to help increase your self awareness and support your progress. You can also use the TICES log to keep track of how you feel in between sessions.

Today's Date: _____

Theme/Experience I worked on today:

Time Period I'm working on:

- ☐ Past
- ☐ Present
- ☐ Future

_____

_____

_____

_____

### How do you feel after today's session?

_____

_____

### Was anything challenging/difficult about today's session?

_____

_____

### Resources that can help me in between sessions?

_____

_____

## *Notes*

### Other insights from today?

_____

_____

# *Reprocessing*
# SESSION SUMMARY

Use this form after each reprocessing session to help increase your self awareness and support your progress. You can also use the TICES log to keep track of how you feel in between sessions.

Today's Date: _____    Theme/Experience I worked on today:

Time Period I'm working on:

☐ Past

☐ Present

☐ Future

### How do you feel after today's session?

_____

_____

### Was anything challenging/difficult about today's session?

_____

_____

### Resources that can help me in between sessions?

_____

_____

## *Notes*

### Other insights from today?

_____

_____

# *Reprocessing*
# SESSION SUMMARY

Use this form after each reprocessing session to help increase your self awareness and support your progress. You can also use the TICES log to keep track of how you feel in between sessions.

Today's Date: _____

Theme/Experience I worked on today:

Time Period I'm working on:

☐ Past

☐ Present

☐ Future

_____

_____

_____

### How do you feel after today's session?

_____

_____

### Was anything challenging/difficult about today's session?

_____

_____

### Resources that can help me in between sessions?

_____

_____

## *Notes*

### Other insights from today?

_____

_____

*Reprocessing*

# SESSION SUMMARY

Use this form after each reprocessing session to help increase your self awareness and support your progress. You can also use the TICES log to keep track of how you feel in between sessions.

Today's Date: _____

Theme/Experience I worked on today:

Time Period I'm working on:

_____

☐ Past

_____

☐ Present

_____

☐ Future

### How do you feel after today's session?

_____
_____

### Was anything challenging/difficult about today's session?

_____
_____

### Resources that can help me in between sessions?

_____
_____

*Notes*

### Other insights from today?

_____
_____

# *Reprocessing*
# SESSION SUMMARY

Use this form after each reprocessing session to help increase your self awareness and support your progress. You can also use the TICES log to keep track of how you feel in between sessions.

Today's Date: _____     Theme/Experience I worked on today:

Time Period I'm working on:

☐ Past

☐ Present

☐ Future

### How do you feel after today's session?

_____

_____

### Was anything challenging/difficult about today's session?

_____

_____

### Resources that can help me in between sessions?

_____

_____

## *Notes*

### Other insights from today?

_____

_____

# *Reprocessing*
# SESSION SUMMARY

Use this form after each reprocessing session to help increase your self awareness and support your progress. You can also use the TICES log to keep track of how you feel in between sessions.

Today's Date: _____

Theme/Experience I worked on today:

Time Period I'm working on:

_____

☐ Past

_____

☐ Present

_____

☐ Future

_____

### How do you feel after today's session?

_____

_____

### Was anything challenging/difficult about today's session?

_____

_____

### Resources that can help me in between sessions?

_____

_____

## *Notes*

Other insights from today?

_____

_____

# *Reprocessing*
# SESSION SUMMARY

Use this form after each reprocessing session to help increase your self awareness and support your progress. You can also use the TICES log to keep track of how you feel in between sessions.

Today's Date: _____

Theme/Experience I worked on today:

Time Period I'm working on:

_____

☐ Past

_____

☐ Present

_____

☐ Future

_____

## How do you feel after today's session?

_____

_____

## Was anything challenging/difficult about today's session?

_____

_____

## Resources that can help me in between sessions?

_____

_____

## *Notes*

### Other insights from today?

_____

_____

*Reprocessing*

# SESSION SUMMARY

Use this form after each reprocessing session to help increase your self awareness and support your progress. You can also use the TICES log to keep track of how you feel in between sessions.

Today's Date: _____     Theme/Experience I worked on today:

Time Period I'm working on:

☐ Past

☐ Present

☐ Future

How do you feel after today's session?

_____

_____

Was anything challenging/difficult about today's session?

_____

_____

Resources that can help me in between sessions?

_____

_____

*Notes*

Other insights from today?

_____

_____

# *Reprocessing*
# SESSION SUMMARY

Use this form after each reprocessing session to help increase your self awareness and support your progress. You can also use the TICES log to keep track of how you feel in between sessions.

Today's Date: _____

Theme/Experience I worked on today:

Time Period I'm working on:

☐ Past

☐ Present

☐ Future

_____

_____

_____

_____

### How do you feel after today's session?

_____

_____

### Was anything challenging/difficult about today's session?

_____

_____

### Resources that can help me in between sessions?

_____

_____

## *Notes*

### Other insights from today?

_____

_____

*Reprocessing*

# SESSION SUMMARY

Use this form after each reprocessing session to help increase your self awareness and support your progress. You can also use the TICES log to keep track of how you feel in between sessions.

Today's Date: _____

Theme/Experience I worked on today:

Time Period I'm working on:

_____

☐ Past

_____

☐ Present

_____

☐ Future

### How do you feel after today's session?

_____

_____

### Was anything challenging/difficult about today's session?

_____

_____

### Resources that can help me in between sessions?

_____

_____

*Notes*

Other insights from today?

_____

_____

# *Reprocessing*
# SESSION SUMMARY

Use this form after each reprocessing session to help increase your self awareness and support your progress. You can also use the TICES log to keep track of how you feel in between sessions.

Today's Date: _____     Theme/Experience I worked on today:

Time Period I'm working on:     _____

☐ Past     _____

☐ Present     _____

☐ Future     _____

### How do you feel after today's session?

_____

_____

### Was anything challenging/difficult about today's session?

_____

_____

### Resources that can help me in between sessions?

_____

_____

## *Notes*

### Other insights from today?

_____

_____

*Reprocessing*

# SESSION SUMMARY

Use this form after each reprocessing session to help increase your self awareness and support your progress. You can also use the TICES log to keep track of how you feel in between sessions.

Today's Date: _____     Theme/Experience I worked on today:

Time Period I'm working on:

☐ Past

☐ Present

☐ Future

### How do you feel after today's session?

_____

_____

### Was anything challenging/difficult about today's session?

_____

_____

### Resources that can help me in between sessions?

_____

_____

*Notes*

Other insights from today?

_____

_____

*Reprocessing*

# SESSION SUMMARY

Use this form after each reprocessing session to help increase your self awareness and support your progress. You can also use the TICES log to keep track of how you feel in between sessions.

Today's Date: _____

Theme/Experience I worked on today:

Time Period I'm working on:
_____

☐ Past
_____

☐ Present
_____

☐ Future

### How do you feel after today's session?
_____
_____

### Was anything challenging/difficult about today's session?
_____
_____

### Resources that can help me in between sessions?
_____
_____

*Notes*

### Other insights from today?
_____
_____

*Reprocessing*
# SESSION SUMMARY

Use this form after each reprocessing session to help increase your self awareness and support your progress. You can also use the TICES log to keep track of how you feel in between sessions.

Today's Date: _____

Time Period I'm working on:

☐ Past

☐ Present

☐ Future

Theme/Experience I worked on today:

_____

_____

_____

### How do you feel after today's session?

_____

_____

### Was anything challenging/difficult about today's session?

_____

_____

### Resources that can help me in between sessions?

_____

_____

*Notes*

### Other insights from today?

_____

_____

# *Reprocessing*
# TICES LOG
## *Triggers, Images, Cognitions, Emotions & Sensations*

TICES stands for Triggers, Images, Cognitions, Emotions and Sensations. Use this log in between reprocessing sessions to promote self awareness and any processing may that continues between sessions.

| Trigger/Dream | I/C/E/S | Intensity | Support |
|---|---|---|---|
| What triggered you/dream did you have? | What image, thoughts, emotions, behaviors and/or sensations occurred when you were triggered/in the dream? | How upsetting was it? 0-10 (10 is the worst) | Did you use your resources or find a new one? |
| | | | |
| | | | |
| | | | |
| | | | |

# *Reprocessing*
# TICES LOG
## *Triggers, Images, Cognitions, Emotions & Sensations*

TICES stands for Triggers, Images, Cognitions, Emotions and Sensations. Use this log in between reprocessing sessions to promote self awareness and any processing may that continues between sessions.

| Trigger/Dream | I/C/E/S | Intensity | Support |
|---|---|---|---|
| What triggered you/dream did you have? | What image, thoughts, emotions, behaviors and/or sensations occurred when you were triggered/in the dream? | How upsetting was it? 0–10 (10 is the worst) | Did you use your resources or find a new one? |
| | | | |
| | | | |
| | | | |
| | | | |
| | | | |
| | | | |

# *Reprocessing*
# TICES LOG
## *Triggers, Images, Cognitions, Emotions & Sensations*

TICES stands for Triggers, Images, Cognitions, Emotions and Sensations. Use this log in between reprocessing sessions to promote self awareness and any processing may that continues between sessions.

| Trigger/Dream | I/C/E/S | Intensity | Support |
|---|---|---|---|
| What triggered you/dream did you have? | What image, thoughts, emotions, behaviors and/or sensations occurred when you were triggered/in the dream? | How upsetting was it? 0-10 (10 is the worst) | Did you use your resources or find a new one? |
| | | | |
| | | | |
| | | | |
| | | | |

# TICES LOG

## *Triggers, Images, Cognitions, Emotions & Sensations*

TICES stands for Triggers, Images, Cognitions, Emotions and Sensations. Use this log in between reprocessing sessions to promote self awareness and any processing may that continues between sessions.

| Trigger/Dream | I/C/E/S | Intensity | Support |
|---|---|---|---|
| What triggered you/dream did you have? | What image, thoughts, emotions, behaviors and/or sensations occurred when you were triggered/in the dream? | How upsetting was it? 0-10 (10 is the worst) | Did you use your resources or find a new one? |
| | | | |
| | | | |
| | | | |
| | | | |
| | | | |
| | | | |

# TICES LOG

## *Triggers, Images, Cognitions, Emotions & Sensations*

TICES stands for Triggers, Images, Cognitions, Emotions and Sensations. Use this log in between reprocessing sessions to promote self awareness and any processing may that continues between sessions.

| Trigger/Dream | I/C/E/S | Intensity | Support |
|---|---|---|---|
| What triggered you/dream did you have? | What image, thoughts, emotions, behaviors and/or sensations occurred when you were triggered/in the dream? | How upsetting was it? 0-10 (10 is the worst) | Did you use your resources or find a new one? |
|  |  |  |  |
|  |  |  |  |
|  |  |  |  |
|  |  |  |  |
|  |  |  |  |
|  |  |  |  |

*Reprocessing*

# TICES LOG

## *Triggers, Images, Cognitions, Emotions & Sensations*

TICES stands for Triggers, Images, Cognitions, Emotions and Sensations. Use this log in between reprocessing sessions to promote self awareness and any processing may that continues between sessions.

| Trigger/Dream | I/C/E/S | Intensity | Support |
|---|---|---|---|
| What triggered you/dream did you have? | What image, thoughts, emotions, behaviors and/or sensations occurred when you were triggered/in the dream? | How upsetting was it? 0-10 (10 is the worst) | Did you use your resources or find a new one? |
| | | | |
| | | | |
| | | | |
| | | | |
| | | | |
| | | | |

# *Reprocessing*
# TICES LOG

## *Triggers, Images, Cognitions, Emotions & Sensations*

TICES stands for Triggers, Images, Cognitions, Emotions and Sensations. Use this log in between reprocessing sessions to promote self awareness and any processing may that continues between sessions.

| Trigger/Dream | I/C/E/S | Intensity | Support |
|---|---|---|---|
| What triggered you/dream did you have? | What image, thoughts, emotions, behaviors and/or sensations occurred when you were triggered/in the dream? | How upsetting was it? 0-10 (10 is the worst) | Did you use your resources or find a new one? |
|  |  |  |  |
|  |  |  |  |
|  |  |  |  |
|  |  |  |  |

*Reprocessing*

# TICES LOG

## *Triggers, Images, Cognitions, Emotions & Sensations*

TICES stands for Triggers, Images, Cognitions, Emotions and Sensations. Use this log in between reprocessing sessions to promote self awareness and any processing may that continues between sessions.

| Trigger/Dream | I/C/E/S | Intensity | Support |
|---|---|---|---|
| What triggered you/dream did you have? | What image, thoughts, emotions, behaviors and/or sensations occurred when you were triggered/in the dream? | How upsetting was it? 0-10 (10 is the worst) | Did you use your resources or find a new one? |
| | | | |
| | | | |
| | | | |
| | | | |
| | | | |
| | | | |

# TICES LOG

## *Triggers, Images, Cognitions, Emotions & Sensations*

TICES stands for Triggers, Images, Cognitions, Emotions and Sensations. Use this log in between reprocessing sessions to promote self awareness and any processing may that continues between sessions.

| Trigger/Dream | I/C/E/S | Intensity | Support |
|---|---|---|---|
| What triggered you/dream did you have? | What image, thoughts, emotions, behaviors and/or sensations occurred when you were triggered/in the dream? | How upsetting was it? 0-10 (10 is the worst) | Did you use your resources or find a new one? |
| | | | |
| | | | |
| | | | |
| | | | |
| | | | |

# *Reprocessing*
# TICES LOG
## *Triggers, Images, Cognitions, Emotions & Sensations*

TICES stands for Triggers, Images, Cognitions, Emotions and Sensations. Use this log in between reprocessing sessions to promote self awareness and any processing may that continues between sessions.

| Trigger/Dream | I/C/E/S | Intensity | Support |
|---|---|---|---|
| What triggered you/dream did you have? | What image, thoughts, emotions, behaviors and/or sensations occurred when you were triggered/in the dream? | How upsetting was it? 0-10 (10 is the worst) | Did you use your resources or find a new one? |
| | | | |
| | | | |
| | | | |
| | | | |
| | | | |
| | | | |

# TICES LOG

## *Triggers, Images, Cognitions, Emotions & Sensations*

TICES stands for Triggers, Images, Cognitions, Emotions and Sensations. Use this log in between reprocessing sessions to promote self awareness and any processing may that continues between sessions.

| Trigger/Dream | I/C/E/S | Intensity | Support |
|---|---|---|---|
| What triggered you/dream did you have? | What image, thoughts, emotions, behaviors and/or sensations occurred when you were triggered/in the dream? | How upsetting was it? 0-10 (10 is the worst) | Did you use your resources or find a new one? |
| | | | |
| | | | |
| | | | |
| | | | |
| | | | |

*Reprocessing*

# TICES LOG

## *Triggers, Images, Cognitions, Emotions & Sensations*

TICES stands for Triggers, Images, Cognitions, Emotions and Sensations. Use this log in between reprocessing sessions to promote self awareness and any processing may that continues between sessions.

| Trigger/Dream | I/C/E/S | Intensity | Support |
|---|---|---|---|
| What triggered you/dream did you have? | What image, thoughts, emotions, behaviors and/or sensations occurred when you were triggered/in the dream? | How upsetting was it? 0–10 (10 is the worst) | Did you use your resources or find a new one? |
| | | | |
| | | | |
| | | | |
| | | | |
| | | | |
| | | | |

# *Reprocessing*
# TICES LOG
## *Triggers, Images, Cognitions, Emotions & Sensations*

TICES stands for Triggers, Images, Cognitions, Emotions and Sensations. Use this log in between reprocessing sessions to promote self awareness and any processing may that continues between sessions.

| Trigger/Dream | I/C/E/S | Intensity | Support |
|---|---|---|---|
| What triggered you/dream did you have? | What image, thoughts, emotions, behaviors and/or sensations occurred when you were triggered/in the dream? | How upsetting was it? 0-10 (10 is the worst) | Did you use your resources or find a new one? |
| | | | |
| | | | |
| | | | |
| | | | |

# *Reprocessing*
# TICES LOG
## *Triggers, Images, Cognitions, Emotions & Sensations*

TICES stands for Triggers, Images, Cognitions, Emotions and Sensations. Use this log in between reprocessing sessions to promote self awareness and any processing may that continues between sessions.

| Trigger/Dream | I/C/E/S | Intensity | Support |
|---|---|---|---|
| What triggered you/dream did you have? | What image, thoughts, emotions, behaviors and/or sensations occurred when you were triggered/in the dream? | How upsetting was it? 0-10 (10 is the worst) | Did you use your resources or find a new one? |
| | | | |
| | | | |
| | | | |
| | | | |
| | | | |

# *Reprocessing*
# TICES LOG
## *Triggers, Images, Cognitions, Emotions & Sensations*

TICES stands for Triggers, Images, Cognitions, Emotions and Sensations. Use this log in between reprocessing sessions to promote self awareness and any processing may that continues between sessions.

| Trigger/Dream | I/C/E/S | Intensity | Support |
|---|---|---|---|
| What triggered you/dream did you have? | What image, thoughts, emotions, behaviors and/or sensations occurred when you were triggered/in the dream? | How upsetting was it? 0-10 (10 is the worst) | Did you use your resources or find a new one? |
| | | | |
| | | | |
| | | | |
| | | | |

# *Reprocessing*
# TICES LOG
## *Triggers, Images, Cognitions, Emotions & Sensations*

TICES stands for Triggers, Images, Cognitions, Emotions and Sensations. Use this log in between reprocessing sessions to promote self awareness and any processing may that continues between sessions.

| Trigger/Dream | I/C/E/S | Intensity | Support |
|---|---|---|---|
| What triggered you/dream did you have? | What image, thoughts, emotions, behaviors and/or sensations occurred when you were triggered/in the dream? | How upsetting was it? 0-10 (10 is the worst) | Did you use your resources or find a new one? |
| | | | |
| | | | |
| | | | |
| | | | |
| | | | |
| | | | |

# *Reprocessing*
# TICES LOG
## *Triggers, Images, Cognitions, Emotions & Sensations*

TICES stands for Triggers, Images, Cognitions, Emotions and Sensations. Use this log in between reprocessing sessions to promote self awareness and any processing may that continues between sessions.

| Trigger/Dream | I/C/E/S | Intensity | Support |
|---|---|---|---|
| What triggered you/dream did you have? | What image, thoughts, emotions, behaviors and/or sensations occurred when you were triggered/in the dream? | How upsetting was it? 0-10 (10 is the worst) | Did you use your resources or find a new one? |
|  |  |  |  |
|  |  |  |  |
|  |  |  |  |
|  |  |  |  |
|  |  |  |  |

*Reprocessing*

# TICES LOG

## *Triggers, Images, Cognitions, Emotions & Sensations*

TICES stands for Triggers, Images, Cognitions, Emotions and Sensations. Use this log in between reprocessing sessions to promote self awareness and any processing may that continues between sessions.

| Trigger/Dream | I/C/E/S | Intensity | Support |
|---|---|---|---|
| What triggered you/dream did you have? | What image, thoughts, emotions, behaviors and/or sensations occurred when you were triggered/in the dream? | How upsetting was it? 0-10 (10 is the worst) | Did you use your resources or find a new one? |
| | | | |
| | | | |
| | | | |
| | | | |
| | | | |
| | | | |
| | | | |

# *Reprocessing*
# TICES LOG
## *Triggers, Images, Cognitions, Emotions & Sensations*

TICES stands for Triggers, Images, Cognitions, Emotions and Sensations. Use this log in between reprocessing sessions to promote self awareness and any processing may that continues between sessions.

| Trigger/Dream | I/C/E/S | Intensity | Support |
|---|---|---|---|
| What triggered you/dream did you have? | What image, thoughts, emotions, behaviors and/or sensations occurred when you were triggered/in the dream? | How upsetting was it? 0-10 (10 is the worst) | Did you use your resources or find a new one? |
| | | | |
| | | | |
| | | | |
| | | | |
| | | | |
| | | | |

*Reprocessing*

# TICES LOG

## *Triggers, Images, Cognitions, Emotions & Sensations*

TICES stands for Triggers, Images, Cognitions, Emotions and Sensations. Use this log in between reprocessing sessions to promote self awareness and any processing may that continues between sessions.

| Trigger/Dream | I/C/E/S | Intensity | Support |
|---|---|---|---|
| What triggered you/dream did you have? | What image, thoughts, emotions, behaviors and/or sensations occurred when you were triggered/in the dream? | How upsetting was it? 0-10 (10 is the worst) | Did you use your resources or find a new one? |
| | | | |
| | | | |
| | | | |
| | | | |
| | | | |
| | | | |

# *Reprocessing*
# REFLECTIONS

Directions: Use this form each time you complete a target/finish reprocessing a memory or time period.  A target is complete when your SUD level is 0, your VoC is 7, and you have a clear body scan.

**TARGET/TIME PERIOD**
**I COMPLETED:** _____
_____

### *Differences*

Ways my life is
now different:

_____
_____
_____
_____
_____
_____

### *Insight*

Insights from
processing this target:

_____
_____
_____
_____
_____

### *My challenges*

Processing was difficult at times but, I was able to persevere by...

_____
_____

# *Reprocessing*
# REFLECTIONS

Directions: Use this form each time you complete a target/finish reprocessing a memory or time period.  A target is complete when your SUD level is 0, your VoC is 7, and you have a clear body scan.

**TARGET/TIME PERIOD**
**I COMPLETED:** _____

## *Differences*

### Ways my life is now different:

_____
_____
_____
_____
_____

## *Insight*

### Insights from processing this target:

_____
_____
_____
_____
_____

## *My challenges*

Processing was difficult at times but, I was able to persevere by...

_____

_____

# *Reprocessing*
# REFLECTIONS

Directions: Use this form each time you complete a target/finish reprocessing a memory or time period. A target is complete when your SUD level is 0, your VoC is 7, and you have a clear body scan.

**TARGET/TIME PERIOD
I COMPLETED:** _____

## *Differences*

### Ways my life is now different:

_____
_____
_____
_____
_____

## *Insight*

### Insights from processing this target:

_____
_____
_____
_____
_____

## *My challenges*

Processing was difficult at times but, I was able to persevere by...

_____
_____

# *Reprocessing*
# REFLECTIONS

Directions: Use this form each time you complete a target/finish reprocessing a memory or time period.  A target is complete when your SUD level is 0, your VoC is 7, and you have a clear body scan.

**TARGET/TIME PERIOD
I COMPLETED:** _____
_____

### *Differences*

Ways my life is
now different:

_____

_____

_____

_____

_____

### *Insight*

Insights from
processing this target:

_____

_____

_____

_____

_____

### *My challenges*

Processing was difficult at times but, I was able to persevere by...

_____

_____

# *Reprocessing*
# REFLECTIONS

Directions: Use this form each time you complete a target/finish reprocessing a memory or time period. A target is complete when your SUD level is 0, your VoC is 7, and you have a clear body scan.

**TARGET/TIME PERIOD I COMPLETED:** _____

## *Differences*

Ways my life is
now different:

_____

_____

_____

_____

_____

## *Insight*

Insights from
processing this target:

_____

_____

_____

_____

_____

## *My challenges*

Processing was difficult at times but, I was able to persevere by...

_____

_____

# *Reprocessing*
# REFLECTIONS

Directions: Use this form each time you complete a target/finish reprocessing a memory or time period.  A target is complete when your SUD level is 0, your VoC is 7, and you have a clear body scan.

**TARGET/TIME PERIOD
I COMPLETED:** _____

## *Differences*

Ways my life is
now different:

_____

_____

_____

_____

_____

_____

## *Insight*

Insights from
processing this target:

_____

_____

_____

_____

_____

_____

## *My challenges*

Processing was difficult at times but, I was able to persevere by...

_____

_____

# *Reprocessing*
# REFLECTIONS

Directions: Use this form each time you complete a target/finish reprocessing a memory or time period. A target is complete when your SUD level is 0, your VoC is 7, and you have a clear body scan.

**TARGET/TIME PERIOD
I COMPLETED:** _____

### *Differences*

Ways my life is
now different:

_____

_____

_____

_____

_____

### *Insight*

Insights from
processing this target:

_____

_____

_____

_____

_____

### *My challenges*

Processing was difficult at times but, I was able to persevere by...

_____

_____

# *Reprocessing*
# REFLECTIONS

Directions: Use this form each time you complete a target/finish reprocessing a memory or time period.  A target is complete when your SUD level is 0, your VoC is 7, and you have a clear body scan.

**TARGET/TIME PERIOD**
**I COMPLETED:** _____

## *Differences*

Ways my life is
now different:

_____

_____

_____

_____

_____

## *Insight*

Insights from
processing this target:

_____

_____

_____

_____

_____

## *My challenges*

Processing was difficult at times but, I was able to persevere by...

_____

_____

# *Reprocessing*
# REFLECTIONS

Directions: Use this form each time you complete a target/finish reprocessing a memory or time period.  A target is complete when your SUD level is 0, your VoC is 7, and you have a clear body scan.

**TARGET/TIME PERIOD
I COMPLETED:** _____
_____

## *Differences*

Ways my life is
now different:

_____
_____
_____
_____
_____
_____

## *Insight*

Insights from
processing this target:

_____
_____
_____
_____
_____

## *My challenges*

Processing was difficult at times but, I was able to persevere by...

_____
_____

# *Reprocessing*
# REFLECTIONS

Directions: Use this form each time you complete a target/finish reprocessing a memory or time period.  A target is complete when your SUD level is 0, your VoC is 7, and you have a clear body scan.

TARGET/TIME PERIOD
I COMPLETED: _____

## *Differences*

Ways my life is
now different:

_____

_____

_____

_____

_____

## *Insight*

Insights from
processing this target:

_____

_____

_____

_____

_____

## *My challenges*

Processing was difficult at times but, I was able to persevere by...

_____

_____

_____

# *Reprocessing*
# REFLECTIONS

Directions: Use this form each time you complete a target/finish reprocessing a memory or time period. A target is complete when your SUD level is 0, your VoC is 7, and you have a clear body scan.

**TARGET/TIME PERIOD I COMPLETED:** _____

## *Differences*

Ways my life is now different:

_____

_____

_____

_____

_____

_____

## *Insight*

Insights from processing this target:

_____

_____

_____

_____

_____

## *My challenges*

Processing was difficult at times but, I was able to persevere by...

_____

_____

# Reprocessing
# REFLECTIONS

Directions: Use this form each time you complete a target/finish reprocessing a memory or time period.  A target is complete when your SUD level is 0, your VoC is 7, and you have a clear body scan.

**TARGET/TIME PERIOD
I COMPLETED:** _____

_____

## Differences

Ways my life is
now different:

_____

_____

_____

_____

_____

## Insight

Insights from
processing this target:

_____

_____

_____

_____

_____

## My challenges

Processing was difficult at times but, I was able to persevere by...

_____

_____

*Graduation*

# YOU DID IT!

Congratulations! You made it to the finish line and completed your journey with EMDR Therapy! Take some time to reflect on your journey and how your life is now different. And don't forget to add your graduation date to the cover page in the beginning of this book!

# *Graduation*
# THERAPY REFLECTIONS

Directions: Use this form to reflect on your entire journey with EMDR Therapy.

## *Differences*

Ways my life is
now different:

_____

_____

_____

_____

_____

## *Insights*

Insights from
my experience are:

_____

_____

_____

_____

_____

## *My Hopeful Future*

What are you now looking forward to in your future?

_____

_____

_____

_____

_____

_____

_____

# THERAPY REFLECTIONS

*Graduation*

*My support systems*

People, places and things that can help when I need support are:

_____

_____

_____

_____

_____

_____

*It's important for me to remembner...*

Reflect on anything else that is important to you.

_____

_____

_____

_____

_____

_____

# I NOW HAVE LESS...

Directions: Reflect back on what you wrote before you started reprocessing and see if you achieved what you wanted LESS of and if there's anything else you want to add.

## Thoughts

Thoughts I NOW
have less of are:

_____

_____

_____

_____

_____

## Emotions

Emotions I NOW have less of/more
in control of are:

_____

_____

_____

_____

_____

## Behaviors

Behaviors I NOW
do less of include:

_____

_____

_____

_____

## Sensations

Sensations in my body I NOW
experience less of are:

_____

_____

_____

_____

*Treatment Achievements*

# I NOW HAVE MORE...

Directions: reflect back on what you wrote before you started reprocessing and see if you achieved what you wanted MORE of and if there's anything else you want to add.

## Thoughts

Thoughts I NOW
have MORE of are:

_____

_____

_____

_____

_____

## Emotions

Emotions I NOW feel more
of/in control of are:

_____

_____

_____

_____

_____

## Behaviors

Behaviors I NOW do
MORE of include:

_____

_____

_____

_____

## Sensations

Sensations in my body I NOW
experience MORE of are:

_____

_____

_____

_____

# CERTIFICATE
## OF ACHIEVEMENT

Proudly presented to

_____
*(your name here)*

on this _____ day of _____ in the year _____
     *(numerical date)*       *(month)*       *(calendar year)*

_____     _____
*(Therapist Name)*           *(other relevant info)*

# CERTIFICATE
## OF ACHIEVEMENT

Proudly presented to

_____
*(your name here)*

on this _____ day of _____ in the year _____
       *(numerical date)*           *(month)*              *(calendar year)*

_____      _____
*(Therapist Name)*             *(other relevant info)*

# Part Three

# ADDITIONAL

# INFORMATION

*FAQs*

# ALL THINGS EMDR THERAPY

Read on to learn the answers to some of the most commonly asked questions in EMDR Therapy

# ANSWERED

**WHAT DOES EMDR STAND FOR?**

EMDR stands for Eye Movement Desensitization and Reprocessing.

**HOW DO I KNOW EMDR THERAPY IS RIGHT FOR ME?**

EMDR is designed to treat the past experiences that are contributing to the symptoms that you're experiencing in the present. If you can't recall things from the past that may be associated with what you're struggling with, that's okay! The EMDR therapist will help you make those connections in the history taking process.

If you are struggling with some of the symptoms below, EMDR may be able to help:

- Anxiety, panic attacks, and phobias
- Chronic Pain
- Treatment resistant depression
- Dissociative disorders
- Eating disorders
- Grief and loss
- Performance anxiety
- Personality disorders (common in survivors of complex trauma)
- PTSD and other trauma and stress-related issues
- Sexual assault
- Sleep disturbance
- Substance abuse and addiction
- Violence and abuse

**HOW IS EMDR EFFECTIVE?**

For EMDR to be most effective, self-awareness is very important. This is because you have to be aware of your inner experience, such as your own beliefs, emotions, and sensations in your body.

This doesn't mean if you're not self-aware, you can't get started with EMDR. You just have to be willing to do the work to develop this awareness, which is what some aspects of phase 2 of EMDR help to do.

# ANSWERED

Visit the section on *Phase 2 Resourcing* for more information.

**CAN YOU TAKE MEDICATION WHEN UNDERGOING EMDR THERAPY?***
If you are currently taking prescribed medications, make sure you discuss with your therapist about it. Many individuals who undergo EMDR therapy are also taking medications and are still able to get the same, great results. It is important to remember that everyone is different, though, so **always** speak with your therapist and prescribing physician **first** before making any changes to your medication regimen.

- **Benzodiazepines:** if you are taking any benzodiazepines (xanax, valium, etc.) it is generally recommended to NOT take any on the day of a reprocessing session, before or after. These medications may dull the effects of the reprocessing or make it less effective.

- **Marijuana:** The jury is still out on what the right answer is to this in regards to EMDR Therapy, so you may hear conflicting opinions, but the general rule is the same as benzodiazepines. Since cannabis affects your nervous system, it may also impact the efficacy of the EMDR processing, so it's best practice to not have any before or after your session on the day you see your therapist. That being said, for some individuals, marijuana use may make it easier to break down the dissociative barriers that can get in the way of full reprocessing. Again, communication is what's most important - so talk to your therapist and your physician first to see what the best approach is for you.

- Inform your therapist if any changes to your medication regimen changes. if there are changes in medications or dosage, reprocessing sessions may be put on hold for 1-2 weeks until your nervous system has fully adjusted to the new regimen.

- In some cases, the current medication regimen may make it difficult for an individual to reach the optimal level of arousal needed for EMDR Processing to be done effectively.

This is why it's best practice to share your list of medications with your therapist and sign release forms so that your therapist and prescribing doctor can speak with one another. This will help all of you to come up with a plan that will support your long term goals, while keeping you as comfortable as possible.

*This information is intended to for educational purposes only and in no way is to be perceived as medical advice. Please consult with a physician if you have questions regarding medication.

## WHAT IF I DON'T WANT TO REVISIT EARLY CHILDHOOD MEMORIES?

EMDR is designed to link the past to the present. That being said, some individuals prefer just to focus on the present day/more recent issues that are causing distress. EMDR can help with those as well; however, the results may vary. When focusing on a more recent distress, EMDR can help to reduce the present day symptoms related to that event; however, those symptoms (such as anxiety) may not completely go away if they are connected to earlier life experiences.

Restricted Processing (EMD/EMDr) helps with symptom reduction. Full reprocessing (EMDR) helps with resolution of symptoms and relapse prevention.

It's important to discuss your goals for EMDR treatment with your therapist so that together, you can create a realistic treatment plan that matches your goals for therapy.

## WHAT IF I CAN'T REMEMBER ANYTHING TRAUMATIC HAPPENING TO ME?

It's not uncommon to have difficulty remembering things from the past. That's because when trauma is incorrectly stored in the brain, it's not correctly encoded into memory, so it would make sense that you have a hard time recalling certain events or details about an event. You may only recall bits and pieces of an event, or have zero recollection whatsoever.

Phases 1 and 2 of EMDR therapy are designed to help you feel calm and safe enough to remember and make connections from the present to the past.

# ANSWERED

It's also important to remember that trauma is not just what happened to you, but what did **NOT** happen to you.

## CAN EMDR HELP WITH DISSOCIATION?

To answer simply, yes. EMDR can be fantastic for dissociative disorders. However, it's extremely important to find an EMDR Therapist that has advanced training in working with this population. Not being properly trained in this area may lead to ineffective EMDR therapy or worsening of present day symptoms.

## IS IT NORMAL TO FEEL WORSE BEFORE IT GETS BETTER DURING EMDR THERAPY?

Everyones' process with EMDR Therapy is uniquely different; however, it is not uncommon for symptoms to temporarily intensify during treatment. EMDR is intended to activate thoughts, feelings, memories, sensations, etc. that you may have avoided or forgotten. Avoidance may bring instant relief, but creates long-term discomfort. The discomfort or worsening of symptoms that you may experience during your process is because you are no longer avoiding; however, this discomfort is temporary.

The skills and tools you established during Phase 2 of EMDR Therapy (Resourcing & Stabilization) help to increase your ability to tolerate that discomfort as best as possible.

## WHO CAN PROVIDE EMDR THERAPY?

EMDR Therapy is a form of psychotherapy, and as such, may only be conducted by LICENSED mental health professionals (LMHC, LPC, LMFT, LCSW, PsyD, PhD, Psychiatric Nurse Practitioner).*

Coaching is not psychotherapy. Coaches should NOT conduct EMDR therapy sessions without a license to practice mental health psychotherapy. EMDR Mental Health Therapists have undergone years of education, post-graduate clinical supervision, and have completed a minimum of EMDR basic training (which includes 10 hours of consultation from an experienced EMDR Therapist, known as an Approved Consultant).

## ANSWERED

### HOW DO I FIND THE RIGHT EMDR THERAPIST?

It's important to find a therapist who is grounded and able to attune to your individual needs. Every single person is different, so even though EMDR is a "structured" treatment, being able to modify that structure based upon your needs is a huge part of the process. There are many wonderful EMDR therapists out there, but remember that just because someone is regarded as "great" doesn't mean they are the perfect fit for you.

It can take 1-3 sessions to determine if you and the therapist are a good match together, and if not, that's okay! Don't get discouraged! It is not uncommon to meet with a couple of different therapists until you find the right fit.

*These statements are not to be considered legal advice and only reflect rules and regulations within the United States. Other countries outside of the U.S. may have different regulations. When in doubt, ask a licensed attorney or search the regulations for your area.)*

### ASSESSING THE FIT

A great trauma therapist is one who is mindful and able to tolerate intense emotions, as well as attune to your individual needs. EMDR therapy can activate a great deal of distress and discomfort as part of the process, so a great therapist will be able to sit with you with that discomfort. Doing so allows you to process and heal from the past so you can move forward.

Some questions you can ask when interviewing different therapists include:
- How long have you been practicing EMDR Therapy?
- How often do you use EMDR Therapy in your practice?
- Do you have experience treating (what you'd like to work on) with EMDR?
- Have you done advanced training in EMDR (after basic training)? If so, what are they?
- Do you participate in EMDR Consultation?

Resources to find an EMDR therapist near you include:
- https://www.emdria.org/find-an-emdr-therapist/
- https://parnellemdr.com/members/
- https://maibergerinstitute.com/emdr-therapist-directory/#!directory/map
- Psychologytoday.com

# ANSWERED

## HOW LONG DOES EMDR THERAPY TAKE?

Much like everything else in life, you get out of it what you put into it. Individuals who make a solid commitment to their treatment and regularly practice the tools and skills they learn IN session OUTSIDE of the session tend to achieve results faster.

The frequency and length of your sessions may impact your overall time in treatment. EMDR is NOT talk therapy; therefore, you don't have to have time between sessions so you'll have "stuff" to talk about with your therapist. In fact, emerging research shows that longer, frequent sessions may lead to faster, better results.

Cost is a factor for many individuals so one thing to consider is this: doing EMDR intensively may be costly up front; however, you achieve results faster, therefore, decreasing the total amount you may spend with a therapist long-term.

## CAN I DO EMDR BY MYSELF?

Would you try to do heart surgery at home by yourself or would you feel safer working with a skilled surgeon with a license to practice medicine?

The same is true with regards to EMDR Therapy. EMDR is a form of psychotherapy that is provided by a licensed mental health professional; therefore, it is not recommended to self-administer EMDR on yourself.

While some platforms state that it's safe and effective to do so, it is best to proceed with caution and assess if doing so is in your best interest.

Some of the potential risks involved if you do EMDR at home by yourself, including:

- re-traumatization
- worsening symptoms of dissociation
- intense abreactions (intense emotional experiences associated with reliving a traumatic event)
- ineffective results

# *Frequently Asked Questions*
# ANSWERED

**CAN EMDR BE DONE VIRTUALLY?**

EMDR can be done virtually! In fact, many therapists were conducting virtual EMDR therapy sessions prior to the coronavirus pandemic, which fast-tracked the accessibility of EMDR Therapy for many.

Ways to ensure that you have a positive experience with doing EMDR Virtually with your therapist include:

- Access to a strong internet connection
- Accessibility to a quiet, private space to conduct your sessions in (cars, closets, bedrooms, etc. can all work as long as it's a space that you can feel safe in!
- Headphones (this improves sound quality and is needed if you prefer auditory bilateral stimulation.

*Have another question?*

*Visit*
*theemdrcoach.com*
*for more information on EMDR Therapy*

# *EMDR*
# GLOSSARY OF TERMS

Learn about the most commonly used terms in EMDR therapy.
Your therapist may refer to many of these concepts in your treatment.

# GLOSSARY

### ABREACTION
An abreaction is when a client demonstrates an intense level of emotional disturbance related to a traumatic event. When a client is experiencing an abreaction, it is important for the therapist to assess whether or not the client is within the window of tolerance. An abreaction may sometimes be a release of the repressed emotion related to the target memory, or it can be a sign of hyperarousal.

### ADAPTIVE INFORMATION PROCESSING
Adaptive Information Processing is the foundation of EMDR Therapy. The AIP model states that present day symptoms and behavior are caused by adverse life experiences that are insufficiently processed and stored incorrectly in the brain. Memories are stored by association and form memory networks that link past to present.

### AFFECT SCAN
The Affect Scan can be used to identify memories for reprocessing or during reprocessing. It is useful when explicit memories are not readily available or when clients have difficulty coming up with words or feelings about themselves.

### BACK TO TARGET
Going Back to Target is when the EMDR Therapist redirects a client's focus of attention back to the original memory/experience within a reprocessing session. This is done when a client either looping, if the processing is stuck, or if the client has begun to access adaptive information and the therapist. Only when a client is in adaptive neural networks will the therapist recheck the SUD when going back to target.

### BILATERAL STIMULATION (BLS)
Eye movement, tapping or auditory alternating stimulus used as dual attention stimuli (external focus) while the client simultaneously focuses on some aspect of the internal experience related to the identified target memory.

### BLOCKING BELIEF
A blocking belief is when there is a negative cognition (NC) that is preventing a traumatic memory from resolving to a SUD of zero. Sometimes, the blocking belief may be associated with another memory, known as the feeder memory.

# GLOSSARY

### BODY SCAN
A Body Scan is when a client taps into the physical sensations they are experiencing now when they focus on a traumatic event. The body scan is the last question of the Phase 3 Target Assessment, because it commonly is the most activating for clients.

### CHANNELS OF ASSOCIATIONS
Channels of Association are events, thoughts, emotions, etc., within a targeted memory network that spontaneously arise during reprocessing of the identified target.

### CLINICAL THEMES
Clinical themes are the 3 themes that client's distortions about self typically fall under. These themes are: Responsibility/Defectiveness, Safety/Vulnerability, and Power/Control.

### CLOSURE
Closure is the 7th phase of EMDR Therapy and is done at the end of every session when a target is incomplete. During the closure phase, the therapist must ensure the client's stability and assess for the need of any resourcing or stabilization exercises before the end of the session and to use in between sessions.

### COGNITIVE INTERWEAVE
A cognitive interweave is an intervention that a therapist will use during desensitization when the processing is looping or blocked. Best practice is to choose interweaves or create interweaves that match a client's current level of activation.

### CONSULTATION
The process of meeting with an EMDRIA Approved Consultant or Consultant in Training, either individually or in a group format, to get consistent feedback on your EMDR sessions. Consultation is one of the most effective ways to fully integrate EMDR into your practice and improve your confidence levels in using EMDR.

### DES
The Dissociative Experiences Scale. One of many assessment measures used to evaluate the level of dissociation that a client may or may not be experiencing.

# EMDR
# GLOSSARY

## DIRECT QUESTIONING

Direct Questioning is part of Phase 1, History Taking, of EMDR therapy. This is the process in which you assess for which memories are connected to client's present day difficulties.

## DISSOCIATION

Dissociation is the experience of feeling disconnected from one's body or from one's surrounding. Levels of dissociation that one may experience include: depersonalization, derealization, somatoform dissociation and structural dissociation. Individuals with more severe levels of dissociation require more specialized interventions in order to maintain dual awareness for the reprocessing phases of EMDR Therapy.

## EIGHT PHASES

This refers to the 8 phases of EMDR Treatment. The 8 Phases Include: History Taking, Preparation, Assessment, Desensitization, Installation, Body Scan, Closure, Reevaluation.

## EGO STATES

Ego states are frequently utilized as a preparation method for complex trauma. Identification and co-consciousness of "parts" can be very helpful when reprocessing is stuck or a client is having difficulty with readiness for reprocessing.

## EMD

EMD is desensitization of a single event or part of an event. When utilizing EMD, the focus of treatment is on symptom reduction, rather than reprocessing. When utilizing EMD, you return to target and get the SUD after each set.

## EMDr (EMD Little r)

Restricted Reprocessing. When doing EMDr, the processing is restricting to keep the processing more focused to prevent looping or going into other neural networks of traumatic material.

# GLOSSARY

### EMDR THERAPY

EMDR Therapy is a trauma informed psychotherapy approach. It is based on the principles of Adaptive Information Processing, meaning that present day issues are caused by incorrectly stored upsetting memories from the past. EMDR includes the three prong approach, including the reprocessing of past memories, desensitization of present day triggers and processing of future templates.

### FEEDER MEMORY

A feeder memory is a memory that can often be the cause of when processing is blocked during the Desensitization Phase (phase 4). Feeder memories are typically earlier memories that are contributing to the current level of a disturbance that a client is reporting.

### FLOATBACK

The floatback is part of Phase 1, History Taking. A floatback is a therapist guided process which is designed to access memories that are connected to the present day issue that an individual is coming to counseling for. The floatback is used when associated memories may be out of the individual's level of awareness.

### FUTURE TEMPLATE

The Future Template is the third step of the Three-Pronged Protocol of EMDR. It is designed to enhance an individual's ability to respond adaptively to a situation in the future that is related to the present day issues. It is important to note that the majority of the research on the efficacy of EMDR includes the Future Template, so it is important to make sure this step is not forgotten on your treatment plan.

### HISTORY TAKING

History Taking is Phase 1 of EMDR Therapy. The objective of History Taking is to assess an individual's present day functioning and link to associated memories, determine goals for treatment, assess the clinical landscape and determine skills needed to develop more adaptive responses in present and future situations.

# EMDR
# GLOSSARY

## HYPERAROUSAL
Hyperarousal is when a client is experiencing activation above the window of tolerance, also known as sympathetic nervous system activation or fight or flight. Hyperarousal can be manifested as anxiety, panic attacks, difficulty with regulating emotions or angry outbursts.

## HYPOAROUSAL
Hypoarousal is when an individual is below the window of tolerance, also known as dorsovagal nervous system activation (see polyvagal theory). Hypoarousal is typically manifested as chronic depression, spacing out, numbness, and feeling disconnected from memories or emotional experiences.

## INSTALLATION
Installation is phase 5 of EMDR Therapy. The purpose of Installation is to strengthen the association of the positive cognition to the processed memory.

## LOOPING
Looping is when processing is stalled and an individual keeps circling around the same maladaptive information, and is not able to access adaptive information spontaneously in the processing.

## NEGATIVE COGNITION (NC)
Negative belief of self that is associated with inadequately processed, maladaptively stored negative experiences.

## PERPETRATOR INTROJECT
A perpetrator introject is when an individual inherits the same thoughts, behaviors and frames of reference of their abuser.

## POLYVAGAL THEORY
Polyvagal Theory is the work of Stephen Porges, which discusses different responses from the vagus nerve in response to stress.

# GLOSSARY

Porges' research surmises that we have 3 levels of our nervous system: the Dorsovagal State, the Sympathetic State and the Ventral Vagal State.

## POSITIVE COGNITION (PC)
Positive belief is a more adaptive belief about the self that is identified in relation to the negative belief which is associated with the maladaptively stored negative memory/experience.

## RE-EVALUATION
Re-Evaluation is phase 8 of EMDR Therapy, though it is used at the beginning of every EMDR session when the target was incomplete in the previous session.

## REPROCESSING
Reprocessing is phase 4 of EMDR Therapy. The purpose of phase 4 is to desensitize a target memory and reprocess associated experiences by linking to adaptive information.

## RESOURCING
Phase 2 of EMDR, also known as the stabilization or preparation phase. This is the phase of EMDR that prepares a client for reprocessing of disturbing life experiences. The goal of resourcing is to widen an individual's window of tolerance so they can maintain dual awareness while accessing traumatic material.

## STATE CHANGE
A state change is a temporary shift in one's emotional state facilitated by a change in focus of attention. Example: use of a calm place or breath work to shift from a state of distress to a state of calm.

## STRUCTURAL DISSOCIATION
Structural Dissociation is a form of dissociation seen in chronically traumatized individuals. It is demonstrated as disintegrated parts of the personality.

# GLOSSARY

## SET

A set is typically 20 or more round trip passes of eye movements or other forms of bilateral stimulation (taps, tones) generally used for most clients during reprocessing. Slower & shorter sets of 6-8 are used only during Preparation Phase for installing Safe/Calm Place or other resources. Each individual processes at their own level, so set durations can be modified based on individual needs.

## SUBJECTIVE UNITS OF DISTURBANCE SCALE (SUD 0-10)

The SUD is a scale used to measure the level of distress associated with a memory. 0 is no disturbance or neutral and 10 is the highest disturbance or distress when targeting a memory. The SUD is most commonly used as part of Phase 3 and during Phase 4 of EMDR Therapy.

## TARGET ASSESSMENT

Phase 3 of EMDR. The purpose of phase 3 is to access the target memory experience for EMDR reprocessing by stimulating the current components of the memory. These components typically include the image, belief systems (NC and PC), emotions and body sensations. Rating scales are built into target assessment in the form of the VoC (validity of cognition) and SuD (subjective units of disturbance).

## TARGET MEMORY/ORIGINAL TARGET

The identified memory that is the focus for reprocessing within a clinical session.

## TARGET SEQUENCE PLAN

The Target Sequence Plan refers to the organization of events by age that are contributing to the present day issue. This timeline documents the past, present and future concerns of the presenting problem.

## THREE-PRONGED PROTOCOL

The Three Pronged Approach is the foundation of EMDR Treatment Planning. Processing is done on past events, present day triggers and future templates. EMDR targets are typically processed in this order for full, comprehensive EMDR treatment.

# GLOSSARY

### TICES
TICES stands for trigger, image, cognition, emotion, sensation/SUD. Individuals are often guided to keep a log in between EMDR Therapy sessions, where they keep track of the TICES and associations in between sessions.

### TOUCHSTONE MEMORY
The earliest memory or experience a client can identify that represents the formation of the maladaptively stored memory network.

### TRAIT CHANGE
A characteristic pattern of response or shift in experience that is permanent (versus a temporary shift in one's experience due to the application of a state shift strategy or change in focus)

### VALIDITY OF COGNITION SCALE (VOC 1-7)
The validity of cognition is a measurement of how valid or true the positive belief (PC) feels as one focuses on the Target Memory where 1 feels completely false and 7 feels completely true. It is utilized during Phase 3 of EMDR, Target Assessment.

### WINDOW OF TOLERANCE
The window of tolerance refers to the zone of arousal in which a person can function effectively. Basically, it means that you can feel upset (anxious/scared/etc.), but still be able to function and not be completely hijacked by your emotions. Being above the window of tolerance is usually manifested as anxiety, panic attacks, and angry outbursts.

*Additional Information*

# RECOMMENDED READINGS

For a list of the most up to date recommended books and resources to support your journey with EMDR Therapy, please visit:

**danacarretta.com/books**

# *Additional Information*
# REFERENCES

- Dana, D. (2020). Polyvagal Flip Chart: Understanding the Science of Safety. W.W. Norton & Company Ltd.

- Dana, D., & Porges, S. W. (2018). The Polyvagal Theory in Therapy: Engaging the Rhythm of Regulation. W.W. Norton & Company.

- Felitti, V. J., Anda, R. F., Nordenberg, D., Williamson, D. F., Spitz, A. M., Edwards, V., Koss, M. P., & Marks, J. S. (1998). Relationship of Childhood Abuse and Household Dysfunction to Many of the Leading Causes of Death in Adults. American Journal of Preventive Medicine, 14(4), 245–258. https://doi.org/10.1016/s0749-3797(98)00017-8

- George, C., Kaplan, N., & Main, M. (1985). The Adult Attachment Interview. Google.Com. Retrieved 2021, from http://www.psychology.sunysb.edu/attachment/measures/content/aai_interview.pdf

- Herkt, D., Tumani, V., Grön, G., Kammer, T., Hofmann, A., & Abler, B. (2014). Facilitating Access to Emotions: Neural Signature of EMDR Stimulation. PLoS ONE, 9(8), e106350. https://doi.org/10.1371/journal.pone.0106350

- Lee, E. E., Depp, C., Palmer, B. W., Glorioso, D., Daly, R., Liu, J., Tu, X. M., Kim, H. C., Tarr, P., Yamada, Y., & Jeste, D. V. (2018). High prevalence and adverse health effects of loneliness in community-dwelling adults across the lifespan: Role of wisdom as a protective factor. International Psychogeriatrics, 31(10), 1447–1462. https://doi.org/10.1017/s1041610218002120

- Pagani, M., di Lorenzo, G., Verardo, A. R., Nicolais, G., Monaco, L., Lauretti, G., Russo, R., Niolu, C., Ammaniti, M., Fernandez, I., & Siracusano, A. (2012). Neurobiological Correlates of EMDR Monitoring – An EEG Study. PLoS ONE, 7(9), e45753. https://doi.org/10.1371/journal.pone.0045753

- PhD, P. L., Felder, E., Prichard, H., Milstein, P., & Ewing, N. (2013). Attachment-Focused EMDR: Healing Relational Trauma (1st ed.). W. W. Norton & Company.

# *Additional Information*
# REFERENCES

- Shapiro, F. (2017). Eye movement desensitization and reprocessing (Emdr) therapy, third edition: Basic principles, protocols, and procedures. Guilford Publications.

- Wang, J., Lloyd-Evans, B., Marston, L., Mann, F., Ma, R., & Johnson, S. (2020). Loneliness as a predictor of outcomes in mental disorders among people who have experienced a mental health crisis: A 4-month prospective study. BMC Psychiatry, 20(1). https://doi.org/10.1186/s12888-020-02665-2

# My
# NOTES

# NOTES

_"Trauma is not what happens to us, but what we hold inside in the absence of an empathetic witness."_

_- Peter Levine_

# NOTES

# NOTES

# NOTES

# NOTES

# NOTES

# NOTES

# NOTES

# NOTES

# NOTES

# NOTES

# NOTES

# NOTES

# NOTES

# NOTES

# NOTES

# NOTES

# NOTES

# NOTES

# NOTES

# DANA CARRETTA-STEIN
## MS, LMHC, LPC
### EMDR CERTIFIED & EMDRIA APPROVED CONSULTANT

Dana Carretta-Stein is a licensed mental health counselor and owner of *Peaceful Living Mental Health Counseling*, a trauma informed counseling practice in Scarsdale, NY. Dana's team of therapists help guide their patients through the path of wellness and recovery. They help children, teens and adults of all ages.

Dana is passionate about the importance of trauma informed care and the effect it has on emotional, physical and mental well-being. She loves to learn about and educate others on compassionate, evidence-based, and effective counseling interventions to help individuals of all ages achieve fulfilling relationships and optimal wellness.

Dana is a specialist and avid enthusiast of EMDR Therapy, one of the most effective evidenced based treatments for trauma, and uses it regularly in her practice. As an EMDRIA Approved Consultant, she provides consultation to other EMDR therapists to help them enhance their learning and skills with EMDR Therapy.